BOURBON

WHAT THE EDUCATED DRINKER SHOULD KNOW

by Tim M. Berra

Acclaim Press
— *Your Next Great Book* —

P.O. Box 238
Morley, MO 63767
(573) 472-9800
www.acclaimpress.com

Book & Cover Design: Frene Melton

ISBN: 978-1-948901-13-0 | 1-948901-13-7
Library of Congress Control Number: 2018911846

First Printing: 2019
Printed in the United States of America
10 9 8 7 6 5 4 3 2 1

This publication was produced using available information.
The publisher regrets it cannot assume responsibility for errors or omissions.

DEDICATION

To the memory of my father, Louis H. Berra, who died too soon. He gave me my first sip of bourbon when I was a boy of about 12. Dad drank *Laurel Springs,* and he taught me to make highballs and old-fashioneds. I have fond memories of Dad and my three uncles at family gatherings in the Italian section of St. Louis known as "The Hill". Our extended family was sometimes augmented by Joe Garagiola and Yogi Berra, when they returned to The Hill for feasts on Thanksgiving and Christmas Eve. Jokes were told in Italian with great drama and hand gestures, over piles of homemade ravioli, turkey, ham, and locally made salami. What great times for a boy to experience!

CONTENTS

Preface. 7

An Introduction to Bourbon 8

A History of Bourbon. 22

The Process of Making Bourbon 42

Cooperage and the Perfect Barrel 78

Good Bourbon Needs Time to Mature 94

Bottling Basics. 114

Summary 124

Glossary of Terms 130

Distilleries 166

References. 190

Notes and Further Explanations 196

Acknowledgments. 218

About the Author 220

Index 222

LABROT & GRAHAM

WOODFORD RESERVE®

DISTILLER'S SELECT

Tim M. Berra
June 20, 2015

KENTUCKY STRAIGHT BOURBON WHISKEY

BATCH BOTTLE
1342   1741

APPROVED BY
MASTER DISTILLER *Chris Morris*

45.2% ALC/VOL (90.4 PROOF) 750 mL

10028403

RE USED FOR THIS EXCEPTION
SPECIALLY SELECTED BY OUR

PREFACE

The idea for this book has been fermenting in my brain for several years. While mulling the idea over and over, I made multiple visits to the distilleries along the Kentucky Bourbon Trail and elsewhere, attended Woodford's Bourbon Academy, took Moonshine University's Executive Bourbon Steward Class, acquired and sampled over 150 bourbons, and read all the bourbon books I could find. Meanwhile, I was giving lectures about bourbon and leading tastings for my friends. After reading all the excellent bourbon books out there (see reference list), it was clear to me that the world did not need another 250-page book about bourbon. However, my PowerPoint presentation was getting many favorable comments, and it was clear to me from the questions I was asked, that there was a need for accurate information to be more widely available and easily accessible.

I've been teaching complex subjects such as biology, human anatomy, ecology, evolution, marine biology and ichthyology to university students for decades. It eventually dawned on me that I could present my PowerPoint lecture as a book. I have distilled the important information into bite-sized bits for easy consumption.

This is really two books in one. The main section contains the basics, sort of a "bourbon for beginners." To get maximum benefit out of what I have presented here, read the Notes and Further Explanations at the back of the book when you read each page of the main section. That is the "advanced course," where I have included extra information that embellishes what is on the individual pages. For example, after reading about "why make whiskey," read the related note for information about the Corn and Cabin Act. Knowledge enhances enjoyment.

Cheers,

Tim M. Berra

Opposite and left: My "dipoma" from Chris Morris's bourbon academy at Woodford Reserve Distillery.

The Whiskey Obsession Festival is the largest gathering of whiskey enthusiasts in North America. It is held in Sarasota, Florida in April. Very small, charred, white oak barrels are available for your personal experimentation from Thousand Oaks Barrel Co. and other suppliers. This one-liter barrel added a woody note to *Ten High* that I stored in it for 30 days. Because of the higher surface area to volume ratio, spirits may age 8-10 times faster than the standard 53-gallon barrel.

AN INTRODUCTION TO BOURBON

WHISKEY

❖ Whiskey is a spirit made from grain, water, and yeast distilled at less than 190 proof and stored in oak containers.

❖ Bourbon, Scotch, rye, Canadian, Irish, and Japanese are all whiskeys.

❖ All bourbon is whiskey, but not all whiskey is bourbon.

WHISKEY VS. WHISKY

Spelling is distiller's choice

❖ "Whisk**ey**" in the United States and Ireland, **except** *Maker's Mark, Old Forester, George Dickel, Early Times* and others.

❖ "Whisky" in Scotland, Canada, and Japan.

SPIRITS, BUT NOT WHISKEY

- ❖ Wine, brandy, cognac (fruit).

- ❖ Rum (sugarcane juice or molasses).

  - ❖ Tequila (agave).

  - ❖ Gin (grain, botanicals, juniper berries).

  - ❖ Vodka (grain, potato, or fruit ethanol, plus water) is a grain neutral spirit (GNS) with no taste or color. Multiple distillations to 190 proof. Outsells whiskey.

WHAT IS BOURBON?

❖ "Bourbon whiskey is a distinctive product of the United States" by act of Congress, May 4, 1964.

❖ Code of Federal Regulations, Title 27, Part 5.22: The Standard of Identity.

❖ The mash bill (recipe) must be at least 51 percent corn.

❖ It must be aged in new charred-oak containers.

❖ No additives except water (no coloring or flavoring).

❖ It must be distilled to no more than 160 proof.

❖ It must enter the barrel at no more than 125 proof.

❖ It must be bottled at no less than 80 proof.

ALCOHOL AND TOBACCO TAX AND TRADE BUREAU (TTB)

❖ TTB is the federal agency that regulates alcohol and tobacco production and labeling.

❖ It's part of the Treasury Department (formerly part of the Bureau of Alcohol, Tobacco and Firearms) and focuses on revenue collection.

❖ The TTB determines what can and cannot be called bourbon, rye, or Scotch in the United States.

❖ Enforces the Standard of Identity.

BOURBON CAN BE MADE ANYWHERE IN THE USA

This beautiful old backbar is newly installed in the Service Bar at Middle West Spirits in Columbus, Ohio. It was obtained through Wooden Nickle Antiques of Cincinnati and dates to 1870s Chicago. It was built by Brunswick Furniture of Cincinnati.

A HISTORY OF BOURBON

WHY MAKE WHISKEY?

- ❖ The Revolutionary War reduced rum and molasses imports. Rye was grown in Maryland and Pennsylvania. Whiskey production thrived and pre-dated the Revolution.

- ❖ In 1776, the Commonwealth of Virginia, which included Kentucky, offered 400 acres to settlers who would build a cabin and farm the land west of the Appalachians.

- ❖ Fertile soil and plentiful water yielded heavy corn crops on new lands.

- ❖ Expanding East Coast populations brought immigrants from grain-distilling cultures such as Scotland, Ireland, and Germany, along with their knowledge and stills. Distilling equipment was part of farming.

- ❖ Whiskey was nonperishable, more valuable, and easier to transport and store than corn.

- ❖ The conversion of surplus corn to whiskey became currency in Kentucky.

WHISKEY REBELLION (1791–1794)

❖ In 1791, Congress imposed the first excise tax on a domestic product (whiskey) to pay for the Revolutionary War, at the urging of Secretary of Treasury Alexander Hamilton.

❖ In 1792, Kentucky entered the union.

❖ Tax collection met violent resistance in Western Pennsylvania in 1794.

❖ President George Washington, a rye distiller, called out the militia; he was the only sitting president to lead troops in battle.

❖ The rebellion collapsed, establishing the federal government's authority to tax and enforce laws.

❖ This led to the establishment of political parties.

❖ President Thomas Jefferson repealed the excise tax.

BOTTLING UP THE WHISKEY REBELLION

HOW DID BOURBON GET ITS NAME?

No one knows for sure!

❖ Louisville was named after Louis XVI in 1778. The Kentucky district of Virginia was named Bourbon for the French royal family in 1785.

❖ The oldest legend says merchants in New Orleans asked for the whiskey invoiced from the Ohio River port of Limestone (now Maysville), in Bourbon County, Kentucky, which made the best whiskey available. Barrels were stamped with county of origin and contents, hence "bourbon whiskey."

- ❖ The earliest use of "bourbon" referring to whiskey was in a newspaper ad in Maysville, Kentucky, in 1821: "bourbon whiskey by the barrel or keg."

- ❖ Another legend says drinkers of aged spirits in New Orleans wanted "Bourbon Street whiskey," which became "bourbon."

- ❖ Further speculation is that "bourbon" was chosen to appeal to the cognac-drinking Francophiles of New Orleans, since cognac is sweet and woody like bourbon. Was it an early example of a marketing decision?

WHAT MADE THIS KENTUCKY WHISKEY SO GOOD?

❖ Barrels were charred internally by small straw fires as part of a process to bend the staves while making the barrel.

❖ Barrels may also have been burned internally to clean them for reuse, remove splinters, or to simulate the French aging process of brandy and cognac, popular in New Orleans.

❖ Whiskey aged during months of kinetic transport by flatboat down the Ohio and Mississippi Rivers or to ports on the East Coast. This gave bourbon color and wood flavors, distinguishing it from clear, unaged whiskey.

FACTORS LEADING TO PROHIBITION

In the early 1900s, the Women's Christian Temperance Union (WCTU) blamed society's ills on alcohol consumption.

❖ Alcohol abuse was widespread in society.

❖ Some business leaders felt sober workers were harder workers.

❖ In 1917, the United States entered WWI, and President Woodrow Wilson ordered distillers to produce only industrial alcohol (190 proof) for munitions.

❖ Grains were needed for the war effort.

❖ Prohibitionists linked the enemy (Germans) to the alcohol industry.

❖ Congress submitted the 18th Amendment in 1917, which banned the manufacture, transportation, and sale of liquor, but **not** its consumption. Supported by three-fourths of the states in 11 months.

PROHIBITION ERA (1920–1933)

❖ In January 1919, the 18th Amendment was ratified and took effect one year later over President Wilson's veto.

❖ The **Volstead Act** provided guidelines for enforcing prohibition.

❖ Alcohol could be legally sold only for medical purposes. Only six distilleries could sell preexisting stocks of this "medicine," but could not distill more.

❖ Naturally, many people immediately fell ill.

❖ Medicinal whiskey kept bourbon alive.

❖ Doctors could prescribe one pint of 100-proof whiskey per patient every 10 days.

❖ In 1929, distilling was permitted for 100 days to replenish the medicinal supply.

PROHIBITION CONSEQUENCES

Deaths from wood alcohol poisoning increased.

- ❖ Enforcement was stronger in rural and Bible Belt areas.

- ❖ Bootleggers, speakeasies, gambling, prostitution, and gangsters increased during the Roaring Twenties.

- ❖ Jobs were lost in the distilling, cooperage, bottling, farming, and tavern businesses.

- ❖ In the 1932 presidential election, in the midst of the Great Depression, this "noble experiment" was declared a failure by both parties; repeal was part of FDR's New Deal.

- ❖ The 18th Amendment to the US Constitution is the only amendment to **limit** the freedom of citizens and the only amendment to be repealed.

ALPHONSE CAPONE
1931 POLICE PHOTOS

WAYS AROUND PROHIBITION

❖ Medicinal whiskey was legally obtained at pharmacies.

❖ Scotch and Canadian whiskey were smuggled into the United States.

❖ Cheap tequila from Mexico crossed into Texas, Arizona, and California.

❖ Rum was run into Florida from the Caribbean.

❖ Bourbon was made in Juarez, Mexico, by the Waterfill and Frazier Distillery, operated by Joseph L. Beam, and smuggled into the United States.

❖ Moonshine was locally made.

❖ By definition, moonshine is a spirit distilled illegally without a government license. What is labeled "moonshine" in a store today is not moonshine. The tax was paid, and it is legal.

PROHIBITION WAS REPEALED BY THE 21ST AMENDMENT IN 1933

❖ On February 20, 1933, Congress proposed a 21st Amendment to repeal the 18th.

❖ Franklin D. Roosevelt was inaugurated on March 4 and proposed changing the Volstead Act.

❖ The 21st Amendment was ratified by states on December 5, 1933. Job creation was a benefit.

❖ The name of *FEW* bourbon is a poke in the eye to the WCTU. It's named after **F**rances **E**lizabeth **W**illard, WCTU president. Born in New York, she later lived in Evanston, Illinois, which remained dry until 1972.

❖ Twenty of Kentucky's 120 counties are completely dry today.

THE CHICAGO DAILY NEWS

COMPLETE MARKETS — TUESDAY, DECEMBER 5, 1933—THIRTY-FOUR PAGES. — COMPLETE WANT ADS — THREE CENTS

EGAL LIQUOR FLOWS TODAY

FINAL EDITION

CHICAGO READY TO CELEBRATE

DRY ERA'S EXIT

Utah Speeds Vote to End Dry Era

Utah Ready to Vote

"DRY ERA" AT END TODAY

ARMED CITIZENS FOIL HUEY LONG; HALT ELECTION

PROHIBITION ENDS AT LAST!

DECEMBER 5, 1933

CELEBRATE!

Antique pot stills, copper condensing coils, and wooden fermenting tank at Evan Williams Bourbon Experience in Louisville, KY.

THE PROCESS OF MAKING BOURBON

AGE REQUIREMENT

❖ There is **no** age requirement. Whiskey aged one minute in a new charred-oak barrel is legally "bourbon."

❖ **"Straight bourbon"** must be aged a minimum of two years in new charred-oak barrels. The age must be listed on the label if it's less than four years.

❖ Bourbon aged four or more years may be called "straight bourbon" without listing an age statement.

❖ The same is true for straight rye and straight wheat whiskeys.

- ❖ The age statement on mingled batches refers to the youngest batch. If the youngest barrel is over four years, no age statement is required.

- ❖ "Kentucky bourbon" must be mashed, fermented, distilled, and aged in Kentucky for a minimum of one year.

- ❖ Most bourbons are four to eight years old.

- ❖ The age is often stated if it's over six years.

- ❖ Unlike wine, aging **stops** when bourbon is dumped from barrel to bottle. A 10-year-old bottled bourbon kept for 10 years is **not** a 20-year-old bourbon.

HOW TO INTERPRET A WHISKEY LABEL

The label must accurately state what is in the bottle and cannot be misleading.

❖ The state name is the location of the distillery.

❖ "Distilled and bottled by" means the brand does its own distilling, e.g., *Ancient Age*.

❖ "Bottled by" means the brand sources whiskey from an unnamed distillery, e.g., *Corner Creek*.

CORNER CREEK
RESERVE BOURBON WHISKEY

AGED IN NEW AMERICAN OAK
DISTILLED, AGED, AND BOTTLED IN KENTUCKY
BOTTLED BY CORNER CREEK DISTILLING CO.
BARDSTOWN, KENTUCKY

44% ALC. BY VOL. (88 PROOF)

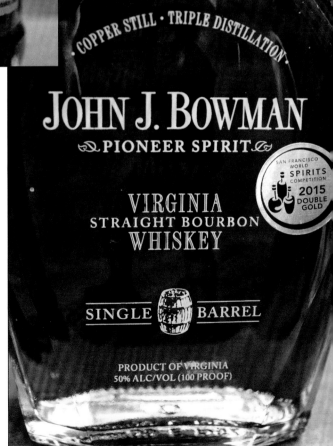

THE MASH BILL
IS THE GRAIN RECIPE

❖ In the bourbon mash bill, most distilleries use about 70 percent corn, about 10 percent barley, and the balance is rye.

❖ A high rye bill has more than 18 percent rye, e.g., 68 percent corn, 28 percent rye, 4 percent barley as in *Bulleit. Four Roses, Old Forester, Basil Hayden's, Woodford Reserve, Old Grand Dad, 1792,* and *Very Old Barton*—all high rye bourbons.

❖ In wheated bourbon, the rye is replaced with wheat, e.g., *Maker's Mark, Weller, Old Fitzgerald, Larceny, Pappy Van Winkle,* and *Rebel Yell.*

❖ Rye is spicier. Wheat is softer and sweeter.

❖ Straight wheat whiskey is at least 51 percent wheat plus corn and barley, e.g., *Bernheim Original.*

❖ Straight rye whiskey is at least 51 percent rye.

CORN WHISKEY IS NOT A SYNONYM FOR BOURBON

❖ By definition, the mash bill of corn whiskey must be at least 80 percent corn.

❖ The range can be 80 to 100 percent corn.

❖ It must be distilled at no more than 160 proof.

❖ It's often not aged. If it's aged, barrels are used or uncharred oak, resulting in light-colored whiskey.

❖ It can be barreled at no more than 125 proof.

❖ Alternative names include corn liquor or white lightning.

BARLEY

Barley is the tertiary grain, after corn and rye or wheat.

- ❖ Barley is malted (germinated) and dried to halt sprouting.

- ❖ This step releases hydrolytic enzymes that catalyze yeast's ability to split starches into simple sugars.

- ❖ Barley adds some flavor.

- ❖ Alberta, Canada, and North Dakota, Montana, Washington, and Idaho are big barley producers.

- ❖ Single malt Scotch is 100 percent barley.

WATER: ANOTHER SOURCE OF FLAVOR

- ❖ Kentucky's karst topography has abundant limestone aquifers and 90,000 miles of streams.

- ❖ Kentucky produces 95 percent of all bourbon.

- ❖ Limestone is a natural filter; it removes iron that would blacken bourbon.

- ❖ Limestone adds $CaCO_3$, necessary for pH control of fermentation.

- ❖ Calcium and magnesium in the water are also nutrients used by the yeast in fermentation.

Batch
22

COOKING

Cooking sterilizes the mash and makes starch soluble.

❖ The corn is locally sourced, inspected for mold and cracks, dried, milled into powder, and boiled with local water to release starches from the grain.

❖ The corn mash is cooled to about 190°F (88°C) and rye or wheat is added to cook about 10 minutes.

❖ After cooling to about 145°F (63°C), malted barley is added and enzymes from barley convert starches into sugars usable by the yeast during fermentation.

SETBACK/BACKSET

Setback is the thin liquid of spent mash and dead yeast from previous distillation.

- ❖ **Setback** (as much as 25–33 percent by volume) is pumped from the beer still to the cooker (mash tub).

- ❖ This is done to ensure consistency from batch to batch, to lower pH, add nutrients, save water, and prevent contamination by wild yeast.

- ❖ The resulting whiskey is **sour mash**.

- ❖ Most bourbons are sour mash.

- ❖ **Sweet mash** uses **no** setback, e.g., *Stranahan's Colorado Whiskey.*

FERMENTATION

Fermentation is the chemical breakdown of a substance by yeast in which sugars are converted to ethanol, CO_2, and heat.

- ❖ Mash in the cooker is cooled from about 145°F to 70°F (63–21°C) via water coils.

- ❖ The cooled, cooked mash with setback goes into a large tub (fermenter) made of cypress wood or stainless steel.

- ❖ Yeast is added and feeds on sugars, giving off CO_2, heat, alcohol, and fruity-smelling compounds (esters).

- ❖ The temperature must be kept under 90°F (32°C).

- ❖ Temperature controls the timing of fermentation.

- ❖ The result is **distiller's beer** (about 8–18 percent alcohol by volume (ABV) in three to four days as the sugars are used up and yeast stops feeding. ABV 11–18 percent kills yeast.

Batch
25

FERMENTER
#4

7,500 gal.
28,390.6 liters

YEAST: *SACCHAROMYCES CEREVISIAE*

Yeast is a single-celled, living fungus.

❖ Proprietary yeast strains are jealously guarded and protected in multiple refrigerated locations away from distilleries, in case of fire.

❖ Specific strains are used for decades.

❖ *Four Roses* distillery uses five yeast strains and two mash bills, resulting in 10 bourbon recipes, the most in the industry.

DISTILLATION

Distillation is a method of separating mixtures of liquids by boiling and subsequent condensation.

There are two types of stills: column and pot.

❖ A **column** (continuous) still is one to six feet in diameter, several stories tall, with horizontal plates with holes. Distiller's beer is injected a quarter of the way from the top, trickles down the plates, and steam is injected at the bottom, which is hotter than the top.

❖ Temperatures between the boiling point of ethanol (173°F, 78°C) and the boiling point of H_2O (212°F, 100°C) yield ethanol, which vaporizes upward, and is captured and condensed at about 125 proof in the first distillation.

❖ This process can go on continuously as beer is added.

❖ The spent mash and setback flow out the bottom.

- ❖ A **pot still** looks like a pot or gourd (*Willett* bottle).

- ❖ It is heated at the bottom to vaporize alcohol upward to the condensing coil.

- ❖ It can distill only one batch at a time, as it must be cleaned out after each use.

- ❖ Pot stills are used by Scotch and Irish distillers and many American craft distillers.

- ❖ *Woodford Reserve* is the only triple-distilled pot-still bourbon.

- ❖ Other Kentucky distilleries use column stills.

Batch

28

By law, bourbon cannot be distilled higher than 160 proof.

❖ Most distillers do not approach the 160 proof limit except Woodford's triple pot-still distillation: about 158 proof.

❖ The industry average is about 140 proof.

❖ Over 160 proof, too much flavor, aroma, and body are removed from the distillate.

❖ By law, vodka is distilled at 190 proof and is essentially a grain neutral spirit (ethanol) without flavor or color.

❖ The theoretical (azeotropic) limit of ordinary distillation is 95.6 percent ABV (191.2 proof) because the ethanol:water mix has a constant boiling point at 95.6:4.4 ratio. The residual liquid and vapor composition remain identical.

Most stills are made of copper because of excellent heat conduction and removal of sulfur compounds in distiller's beer as copper sulfate ($CuSO_4$).

❖ Distillation removes unwanted compounds (congeners), such as aldehydes, esters, other alcohols, etc. from ethanol.

❖ "Heads" (the first about 5 percent to vaporize) are discarded. Heads are high in nasty stuff such as acetone and methanol, which can kill.

❖ "Hearts" (or "low wine," the best part of the distillate) match the proof and taste profile and are captured and redistilled in the doubler.

❖ "Tails" are fusel oils and low-proof ethanol added back to later distillation to recycle the ethanol.

Batch
30

Spirit Safe or Tail Box

❖ This is where the distiller diverts the "cuts" into holding tanks for re-distillation or disposal.

❖ The distiller redirects and discards the heads, small molecules with low boiling points, such as acetaldehyde, acetone, methanol and ethyl acetate.

❖ The distiller reserves and measures the specific gravity (alcohol content) of the hearts, the good stuff, for re-distillation in the doubler into "high wine" or "white dog".

❖ The distiller captures the tails (the larger molecules with high boiling points, such as butyl alcohol, acetic acid, amyl alcohol, and furfural for recycling distillation to save any ethanol present.

❖ The **low wine** (hearts) from the first distillation is about 125 proof.

❖ This liquid is run through a second distillation in a small pot still (doubler or thumper) for further refinement.

❖ The **high wine** ("new-make," or "white dog") comes from doubler at about 135 proof. It tastes like corn.

❖ After dilution with water, the distillate is put into barrels for aging at **no more** than 125 proof. Some distillers use a **barrel entry proof** from 120 to 103 ⟵ proof, claiming extra water yields a smoother result due to dissolved and oxidized phenols.

❖ Forty-four thousand gallons of distiller's beer yields about 6,000 gallons of white dog.

❖ Spent mash (slop) is spun, dried, and sold to farmers as nutritious livestock feed; it's high in protein.

Barrel Entry Proof

◆ *Beam, Buffalo Trace, Heaven Hill*: 125 proof

◆ *Four Roses* and *Town Branch*: 120 proof

◆ *FEW*: 118 proof

◆ *Wild Turkey*: 115 proof

◆ *W.L. Weller/Van Winkle*: 114 proof

◆ *Maker's Mark* and *Woodford Reserve*: 110 proof

◆ *Michter's:* 103 proof

Charring of white oak barrels at Brown-Forman Cooperage, Louisville, KY.

COOPERAGE
AND THE
PERFECT BARREL

The standard of identity requires bourbon to be aged in new charred oak containers.

❖ The vast majority of barrels are made of white oak, *Quercus alba*, native to the eastern half of North America.

❖ Its wood is dense, close grained, and possesses tyloses, which plug pores and prevent leaks.

❖ It is prized for its sweet, toasty wood sugars.

❖ French oak, Q. *petraea*, is high in tannins and used mostly for wine barrels. Red oak, Q. *rubra*, is porous and leaks readily.

❖ A typical 100-year-old white oak tree yields two barrels.

COOPERAGE

**A cooperage is where the barrels are made.
A cooper is a barrel maker.**

Anatomy of a 53-gallon (200-liter) bourbon barrel:

❖ Thirty-six inches (91.5 centimeters) tall.

❖ About 26–28 inches (66–71 centimeters) circumference at the bilge; 22 inches (56 centimeters) diameter heads.

❖ Thirty-two to thirty-five staves about one inch (2.5 centimeters) thick.

❖ Six steel hoops: 16-gauge, 1.75 inches (4.5 centimeters) wide.

❖ Brown-Forman is the only distillery with their own cooperage and they have created a bourbon to emphasize their barrel-making expertise.

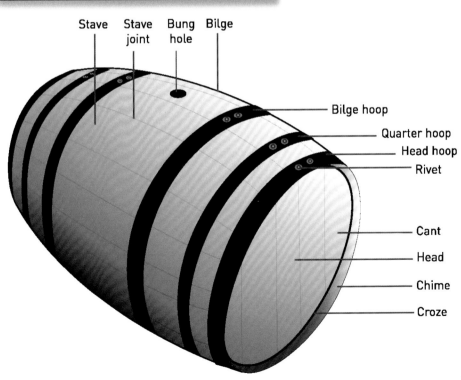

Stave   Stave   Bung   Bilge
joint   hole

Bilge hoop

Quarter hoop

Head hoop

Rivet

Cant

Head

Chime

Croze

- ❖ The Independent Stave Company (ISC), in Lebanon, Kentucky, and Missouri, makes barrels for most distilleries.

- ❖ Aged oak lumber is milled into wide and narrow staves that are wider in the middle and narrower at the ends to account for the curvature of the barrel.

- ❖ Staves are given a specific bevel along their length to fit precisely when bent and ringed.

- ❖ The double-arc design of barrels is very strong and unchanged over centuries.

- ❖ Shorter oak pieces are joined with plugs and cut into a circle for the barrelheads.

- ❖ No glue or fasteners are used.

85

An Art Form

❖ Staves are steam-heated to produce the curvature and held together with temporary steel hoops.

❖ "Raising" a barrel is handwork done by skilled craftsmen who select staves individually to fit together perfectly.

- Barrels are then **toasted** (heated to a specific temperature and time up to two hours) to release molecules from wood such as vanillin and esters from the breakdown of lignin and to caramelize sugars that provide flavor and color.

- Next, barrels are **charred** (fired inside) to the distilleries' specifications. The charcoal lining serves as a filter for undesirable flavors. Barrelheads are also charred.

- ❖ Char levels are from one to four, with four being the deepest "alligator char." Firing time is 25 to 55 seconds. Char three and four are most often used.

- ❖ This cracks and blackens wood and increases surface area which aids whiskey penetration.

Char Levels

1 = 25 sec.
2 = 35 sec.
3 = 45 sec.
4 = 55 sec.

- ❖ After cooling, the barrelheads are fitted into a groove (croze) around the top and bottom edge of the staves and six permanent steel hoops hold the staves tightly together.

- ❖ There are two head hoops, two quarter hoops, and two bilge (center) hoops.

- ❖ Rivets fasten the hoops together and bear the identification of the cooperage. "KY" or "MO" for ISC's two localities or "B" for Brown-Forman.

- ❖ A bunghole is drilled in the center of the widest stave.

Batch

38

BARREL AND BUNG (STOPPER) TRIVIA

❖ Barrels are filled with two gallons of water and pressure tested. Leaking staves are replaced.

❖ Most distilleries use poplar bungs that expand when wet to form a tight seal. *Maker's Mark* uses walnut, which is less likely to splinter since *Maker's Mark* ages "to taste" rather than by years, so the distiller must tap barrels more often.

❖ An empty barrel weighs about 105 pounds (47.6 kilograms); when filled with 53 gallons (200 liters) of whiskey, it weighs about 510 pounds (231 kilograms).

❖ Full barrels can be rolled by one person.

❖ Barrels cost about $170 each.

Rickhouse of Willett Distillery,
Bardstown, KY at sunset.

GOOD BOURBON NEEDS TIME TO MATURE

MATURATION

A rickhouse, rackhouse, and warehouse are the same thing.

❖ Filled barrels are stored in a rickhouse on their sides, cradled in a rick for two to 23 years with the bungs oriented up.

❖ Tiered ricks allow maximum air flow and facilitate movement of the barrels.

❖ Many rickhouses are metal clad, and oriented for maximum sun exposure on the longest sides.

❖ Most rickhouses are unheated (except Brown-Forman and *Buffalo Trace*) and most are six to nine stories tall.

❖ *Four Roses* uses a one-story rickhouse to minimize temperature differential and promote uniform aging.

"Main Street" in a rickhouse.

❖ Barrels are rolled down the main aisle and distributed to the ricks.

❖ A platform elevator is used to lift two to six barrels at a time to higher stories.

❖ Barrels are stacked three high per floor.

- ❖ In summer, the liquid expands into the wood and dissolves caramels and sugars. Ethanol is the solvent.

- ❖ Contraction in winter brings the flavors into the barrel while filtering out harshness via the char.

❖ The temperature differential from the top to the bottom of the rickhouse can be about 35°F (19°C), or only 8°F in a single-story rickhouse.

The barrel produces 100 percent of the color and 50-75 percent of the flavor of bourbon.

❖ Aging in charred barrels produces color and flavor as liquid diffuses into and out of the wood as it expands and contracts over time with temperature changes.

❖ **Incoming air oxidizes compounds to aromatic fruity esters.**

❖ Aging six years or more yields more confection notes from the red layer: vanilla, butterscotch, caramel, cinnamon, toffee, etc. Six to twelve years is the sweet spot.

❖ Excessive aging may result in a too-woody taste.

❖ Time is an ingredient.

The char gives Bourbon its deepening amber color.

The "Red Layer" yields the flavors.

The "soakage" line shows how deep the whiskey has entered the wood.

- ❖ High in the rickhouse, it's hot and dry. The **proof increases** from 125 to about 145 as H_2O escapes faster than ethanol. This concentrates flavors, adds a stronger oak taste, and results in faster aging.

- ❖ In the middle of a rickhouse, where barrels are insulated by thermal mass, proof **fluctuates slightly**, 120 to 130. Aging is uniform and predictable, and there's less wood spice.

- ❖ Low in the rickhouse, it's cool and moist. The **proof drops** from 125 to about 110 as ethanol leaves the barrel faster than H_2O in a cool, humid atmosphere. Aging is slower, mellower; it's the best level for superages.

- ❖ Since bourbons age differently throughout the rickhouse, most distillers combine barrels from high, middle, and low ricks (a practice called "cross-sectioning") to obtain their flavor profile.

- ❖ Single barrel and small batches are often taken from specific levels of the rickhouse.

- ❖ The average rickhouse holds 20,000 barrels or a million gallons (four million liters) of whiskey.

- ❖ *Jim Beam* fills about 1,550 barrels a day and has about 1.9 million barrels aging at any one time.

- ❖ *Maker's Mark* is the only major distiller in Kentucky that relocates barrels.

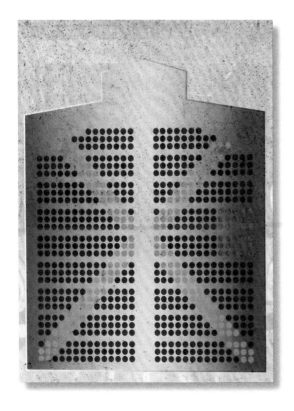

The atmosphere in a rickhouse is heavenly.

❖ Higher floors in rickhouses have higher temps, which means greater evaporation to the "angel's share": 10 percent in the first year, 3 to 4 percent each year after. The yield is 41 gallons for every 53 gallons after four years; 32 gallons for every 53 gallons after nine years.

❖ *Pappy's* 23-year-old yields about 14 gallons out of 53.

❖ Air enters the barrel through the wood, fills the void left by evaporation of the angel's share and oxidizes congeners and acids, thereby enhancing flavor.

109

A WEE DRAM OF CHEMISTRY

Why barrels at the top of the rickhouse age more rapidly.

Water (H_2O)

- Boiling point, 212°F (100°C)
- Molecular weight, about 18.01g/mol
- A small molecule

Ethanol (C_2H_6O)

- Boiling point, 173°F (78.4°C)
- Molecular weight about 46.06g/mol
- A large molecule

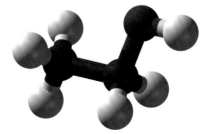

Batch 47

- Molecules move from a region of higher concentration to a region of lower concentration by diffusion.

- In hot and dry conditions at the higher stories of the rickhouse, the concentration of H_2O molecules **outside** the barrel is **smaller** than **inside** the barrel, leading to a greater H_2O gradient between inside and outside and increasing the volatility of the H_2O. Therefore H_2O leaves the barrel and proof increases.

- In cool and humid conditions at lower stories, the concentration of H_2O molecules **outside** the barrel is **larger** than **inside** the barrel, leading to a smaller H_2O gradient between inside and outside and suppressing the volatility of H_2O. More ethanol than H_2O exits the barrel and proof decreases.

WAREHOUSE STAINING FUNGUS

Baudoinia compniacensis

❖ Rickhouses, barrels, even nearby traffic signs are often covered with a black moldy growth.

❖ This highly specialized whiskey fungus feeds on ethanol vapors and has been found in North and South America and Europe where alcohol is distilled.

❖ Its specific Latin name refers to cognac, a product of France.

❖ It is presumed to be harmless to people, other animals, and plants.

Bottling line at Four Roses Bottling
Facility in Cox Creek, KY.

BOTTLING BASICS

BOTTLING

❖ When the flavor profile is reached, the bourbon is dumped, filtered to remove bits of char, and may be chill-filtered to prevent hazy precipitate of proteins and fatty acids. The bourbon is then bottled.

❖ Most bourbons are diluted with demineralized water to achieve the desired 80–100 proof.

❖ *Old Forester* was the first bourbon to be sold in bottles, in 1870.

❖ Used barrels are disassembled, sold to age Scotch, and reassembled as 250-liter casks.

❖ The barrel wall retains about two gallons of bourbon, known as the devil's cut.

- ❖ **Barrel strength** with no added water yields a high proof; typically 110–140 proof, e.g., *Booker's*.

- ❖ **Single barrel** is whiskey bottled from one barrel.

- ❖ **Bottled-in-Bond** [Act of 1897] is whiskey from one distillery made in one season, bottled at 100 proof, and aged at least four years in a government bonded warehouse.

- ❖ **Small batch** is whiskey bottled from mingling of a "small" number of barrels. It's all relative.

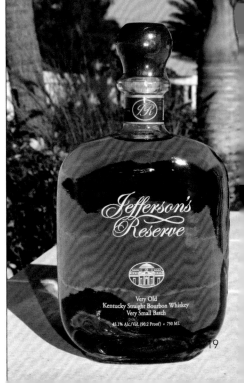

19

BOTTLED-IN-BOND ACT 1897

- ❖ **Rectifiers** were non-distillers who bought whiskey, mixed, and sold their own (often) inferior product.

- ❖ Distiller Colonel Edmund H. Taylor Jr. made quality whiskey and worked to pass this **first consumer protection legislation** with the support of Treasury Secretary John G. Carlisle; the act discouraged rectifiers from adding color and flavor (iodine, tobacco juice, prune juice, creosote, and turpentine) to grain alcohol and selling it as whiskey by creating a "seal of approval" for whiskey made a specified way as described on p 118.

- ❖ President Grover Cleveland signed the act.

PURE FOOD AND DRUG ACT 1906

❖ This act was inspired by horrors of the meatpacking industry exposed by Upton Sinclair in *The Jungle*. President Theodore Roosevelt signed the act in 1906 which barred rectifiers from calling their adulterated product "whiskey".

❖ The act completed consumer protection by defining straight (pure) and blended (imitation) whiskeys.

❖ After much debate in Congress, President William Howard Taft personally decided the meaning of "whiskey" and amended the act in 1909 requiring rectifiers to use the term "blended whiskey". The **Taft decision** allowed "bourbon" or "rye" to be used with "straight whiskey," and helped buyers know exactly what they were getting.

Here is a sight you don't see every day—all six expressions of Van Winkle in one place at the same time. The total list prices for these six bottles is approximately $717. The Ohio Department of Commerce (https://www.ohiolmp.com/brandmaster_public.php) lists the retail prices as follows: *Old Rip Van Winkle 10*, $54.96; *Old Rip Van Winkle 12*, $64.22; *Van Winkle Rye 12*, $99.99 (my estimate); *Pappy Van Winkle 15*, $91.98; *Pappy Van Winkle 20*, $156.80, *Pappy Van Winkle 23*, $249.38. These products are rarely found in liquor stores. The auction value of this collection is about $6,000, half of which is accounted for by the 23-year-old *Pappy Van Winkle*. This "grab shot" was taken at a tasting arranged by Turner C. Moore, the organizer of the Whiskey Obsession, in Sarasota, Florida.

SUMMARY

EACH BOURBON IS UNIQUE DUE TO MANY VARIABLES

❖ Mash bill

❖ Yeast strain

❖ Length and temperature of fermentation

❖ Barrel characteristics and preparation

❖ Entry proof into barrel

❖ Barrel position in the rickhouse

❖ Time in the rickhouse (age)

Modified From Bernie Lubbers's *Bourbon Whiskey: Our Native Spirit.*

Used with permission.

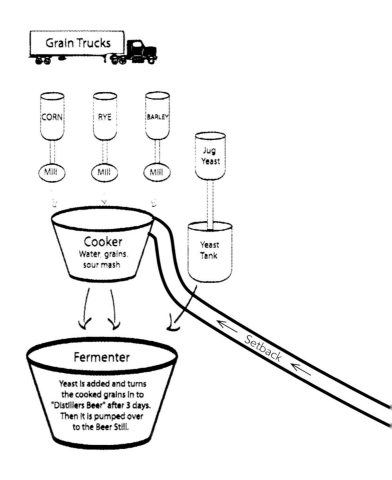

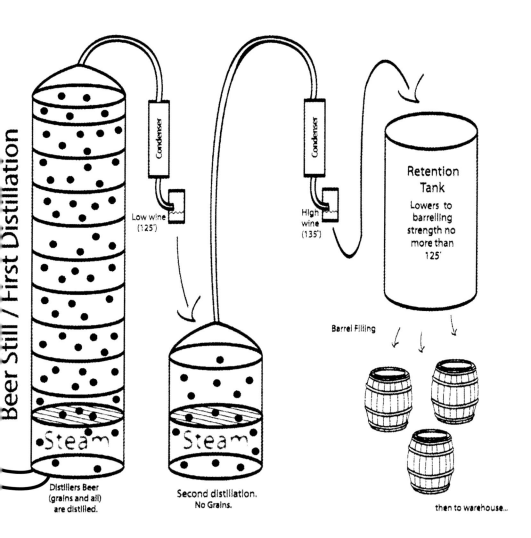

Beer Still / First Distillation

Condenser

Low wine
(125')

Condenser

High
wine
(135')

Retention
Tank

Lowers to
barrelling
strength no
more than
125'

Barrel Filling

Distillers Beer
(grains and all)
are distilled.

Second distillation.
No Grains.

Steam

Steam

then to warehouse...

129

GLOSSARY
OF TERMS

PROOF

In the United States, proof is two times the percentage of alcohol by volume.

❖ A 200-point scale in degrees of proof is used.

❖ A proof of 200 equals 100 percent ABV.

❖ *Wild Turkey* 101 has 50.5 percent ABV.

❖ A proof of 80 equals 40 percent ABV, which is the minimum for bourbon.

❖ A higher proof results from less water and has more flavor.

❖ To test if whiskey has been diluted, mix it with gunpowder. If it burns, it has at least 50 percent ABV.

❖ Origin of gunpowder test lost in antiquity: 16th century English taxation, Royal Navy rum ration test, 19th century cowboy saloon test?

BLANTON'S

Blanton's is marketed as the original single barrel bourbon.

❖ *Blanton's* was released by *Buffalo Trace* in 1984 and is named after the company's former president Albert Blanton.

❖ It's aged in the world's only steam-heated rickhouse (warehouse H).

❖ The *Blanton's* stoppers depict a racehorse and jockey in eight poses; each stopper is marked with a letter, and the full collection of stoppers spells B-L-A-N-T-O-N-S.

❖ *Blanton's* is sold in a unique eight-sided bottle.

IS JACK DANIEL'S TENNESSEE WHISKEY BOURBON?

Yes and no...

- *Jack Daniel's* is the best-selling American whiskey in the world.

- It meets all the requirements for bourbon.

- Tennessee whiskey can be bourbon if it chooses.

- It was a marketing decision to label it Tennessee whiskey.

- *Jack Daniel's* undergoes the Lincoln County Process of mellowing through sugar maple charcoal pellets before barreling. This gravity-fed trickle through a 10-foot column takes about seven days.

- This removes many congeners and produces a very smooth and sweet whiskey.

- *George Dickel* steeps whiskey in a charcoal-filled vat.

The Lincoln County Process
of Charcoal Mellowing
and Tennessee Whiskey

❖ Tennessee whiskey **must** be made in Tennessee.

❖ Bourbon can be made in Tennessee, but Tennessee whiskey cannot be made in Kentucky.

❖ One Tennessee whiskey, *Prichard's*, is **not** charcoal mellowed.

❖ In 2013, at the urging of the Jack Daniel Distillery, a **state** law was passed defining Tennessee whiskey as essentially bourbon that has undergone the Lincoln County Process.

❖ *Prichard's* was the only exemption to this law.

❖ Ironically, the Daniel and Dickel distilleries are not in Lincoln County. *Prichard's* is.

❖ *Dickel* is the second-largest selling Tennessee whiskey, but *Daniel's* outsells it 100:1.

KENTUCKY WHISKEY BUT NOT BOURBON

Kentucky whiskey that isn't bourbon because it is not aged in new barrels.

❖ *Early Times* is the only major American brand that mixes whiskey aged in used barrels (20 percent) with bourbon aged in new barrels (80 percent).

❖ This moderates the stronger flavors of new wood.

❖ It is distilled from a bourbon mash bill but can't be called bourbon.

❖ *Early Times* has a long history and is popular, but it's now considered a bottom-shelf whiskey by some.

MATURED AT LEAST THIRTY-SIX
MONTHS IN REUSED COOPERAGE

10008392

ALSO NOT BOURBON

It is made from a bourbon mash bill but cannot be called bourbon for two reasons.

❖ It is made in Canada, not the United States.

❖ Some of the blended whiskeys are aged in used cooperage.

BLENDED AMERICAN WHISKEY

The term applies to US usage only; it does not apply to Scotch, Canadian, or Irish whiskey.

There are two types:

❖ A combination of different straight whiskeys. This can be very good. If a label says "blended bourbon whiskey," the contents must be at least 51 percent straight whiskey, e.g., *Ten High*.

❖ A combination of at least 20 percent straight whiskey with a younger whiskey or grain neutral spirits. This is inexpensive by definition. The percent of GNS must be on the label. Color, sugar, and flavor are added to simulate the taste, aroma, and look of whiskey, e.g., *Seagram's 7* has 75 percent GNS.

Batch 61

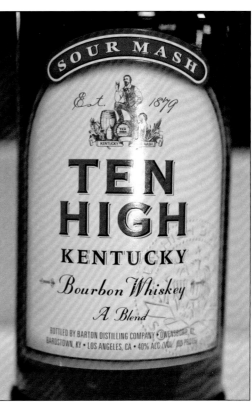

145

FOUR GRAIN WHISKEY

Blended Whiskey

❖ *Oyo* named after the Ohio River valley & produced by Middle West Spirits of Columbus, Ohio.

❖ It is a blend of sourced Kentucky straight bourbon and their own 100% wheat whiskey.

❖ Technically it is not a bourbon since something other than water, namely wheat whiskey, has been added.

Straight Bourbon

❖ Oyo's replacement is a four-grain straight bourbon with a mash bill of 65% corn, 17% wheat, 13% rye, and 5% barley.

❖ *Black Button* Distillery of Rochester, NY. Mash bill of 60% corn, 20% wheat, 9% rye, and 11% barley.

❖ Aged two years in 23 and 30-gallon barrels of 3.5 char level.

SOLERA PROCESS

Fractional blending derived from sherry production and is a process in which a large barrel is repeatedly partially emptied and refilled.

❖ The process is used at Chattanooga Whiskey Experimental Distillery.

❖ A 4000-gallon, #1 charred, new oak solera barrel is filled with a 50/50 blend of 100 barrels of straight bourbon aged two to three years and eight to nine years. The whiskeys are allowed to marry for a length of time, then a small batch (10–15 barrels) is bottled. The solera barrel is then topped off with 10–15 barrels of the straight bourbon 50/50 blend. Drawdown and refilling are repeated again and again. Barrel turnover time is about six months.

❖ This process is said to add complexity and consistency to the final product.

❖ Hillrock Estates in New York was the first to use a variation of this process for bourbon.

The Best of Both Barrels

Solera ➔ Finish

1816 RESERVE IS AN INNOVATIVE UPDATE
TO OUR TRADITIONAL STRAIGHT BOURBON
WHISKEY. UTILIZING OUR OWN VERSION OF
THE CLASSIC SOLERA PROCESS, WE BRING
TOGETHER OVER 100 FULLY AGED BARRELS
OF 1816 INTO ONE LARGE, CHARRED, OAK
SOLERA BARREL. AFTER EACH SMALL BATCH
BOTTLING, WE THEN TOP THE SOLERA WITH
10-15 MATURE BARRELS. THIS CONTINUAL
PROCESS ALLOWS THE WHISKIES TO MARRY
TOGETHER, IMPARTING A GRADUAL
COMPLEXITY OVER TIME.

The Dynamo of Dixie

CHATTANOOGA WHISKEY Co.

1816

RESERVE

Solera Barrel Finished

TENNESSEE STILLHOUSE

90 PROOF

STRAIGHT BOURBON WHISKEY   45% ALC/VOL 375 ML

FINISHED AND FLAVORED "BOURBONS"

- ❖ **Straight bourbon:** only water may be added.

- ❖ **Finished bourbon:** After aging in new charred oak, the bourbon is placed in used wine or beer barrels or non-oak barrels, where it assumes additional flavors: e.g., *Angel's Envy* is finished in port wine barrels.

- ❖ **Flavored bourbon:** Flavoring such as maple syrup, pecan, honey, etc. is added to the bourbon. It must be bottled at no less than 60 proof. This product is **no longer legally a bourbon**, but bourbon is an ingredient on the label. Nevertheless, they can be delicious.

- ❖ All such adulterations must be stated on the label.

ADDING EXTRA "WOOD"

This is a type of finishing (secondary maturation) that does not violate the term "bourbon."

❖ *Woodford Reserve* is dumped into new, long-toasted, lightly charred barrels for about nine additional months and is then labeled *Double Oaked*.

❖ Ten French oak staves are inserted into an existing barrel of *Maker's Mark* for about nine weeks; more tannic acid spices up the whiskey, which becomes *Maker's 46*.

❖ *Prichard's* takes eight-year-old bourbon barreled at 125 proof, cuts it to bottle proof, and ages it again in a second new charred oak barrel to make *Prichard's Double Barreled*.

ATTEMPTS TO SPEED AGING

Terrepure Technology

❖ Developed by Terressentia Corporation in North Carolina, this technology reduces harsh- tasting congeners by using **ultrasonic energy** applied for about six hours to a distillate containing oak staves and added oxygen.

❖ The company claims that it finishes reactions that failed to complete in distillation, and removes methanol, isobutanol, propanol, and amyl alcohols. Harsh acids are converted to smooth esters.

❖ It's said to yield better mouth feel and flavor equal to four to six years of aging.

❖ The company makes whiskey for private labels, e.g., *Chacho* for Columbia Restaurants.

Cleveland Whiskey Speed Aging

❖ Sourced white dog is made to their recipe, aged for a couple of weeks, and sent to Ohio in oak barrels. The white dog and cut-up barrel staves are placed in stainless steel vats and subjected to pressure for 24 hours.

❖ This whiskey is apparently popular in China.

Small Barrel Aging

❖ Some craft distillers use smaller barrels (30, 15, 5, 2 gallons) to increase the surface area to volume ratio and thereby age whiskey faster.

❖ The color is good, but flavor results are mixed.

❖ There is greater evaporation and expense than with 53-gallon barrels.

GLENCAIRN CRYSTAL WHISKEY TASTING GLASS

❖ The thistle shape allows bourbon to open up; the taper at the top focuses aroma for nosing at rim.

❖ The glass was developed in Scotland.

❖ It allows tasters to compare color, body, nose, palate, and finish.

❖ Any glass except a shot glass will do for tasting: rocks glass, brandy snifter, or wine glass.

❖ Add a few drops of water to lower the proof and release flavors if you like.

HINTS FOR BOURBON TASTING

Practice, practice, practice builds up a tolerance to the heat of ethanol.

❖ Color: Hold the glass up and observe the color. Lighter bourbon is younger, lower proof and has a subtle taste. Darker bourbon is older, higher proof, and with a more complex taste.

❖ Body: Swirl the liquid. How does the film or "legs" coat the glass? Thick, thin, short, long? Viscosity affects mouth feel. Thin legs indicate a higher proof; thick legs indicate a lower proof.

❖ Nose: With your mouth open, lower lip at the rim, inhale through your nose and mouth. Note the aroma.

❖ Taste: Take small sips, swirl it around your mouth, "chew." Note the flavor.

❖ Finish: Swallow. Is it smooth or does it burn? If the flavor lingers, it's a "long finish"; if the flavor quickly vanishes, it's a "short finish." Greater age results in a longer finish.

❖ Build a flight. A half ounce equals a 15-milliliter sample: try three to four expressions from low to high proof, or different mash bills or ages.

Batch 68

Legs

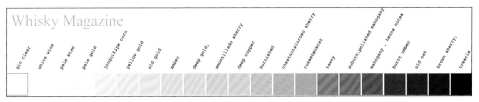

gin clear | white wine | pale staw | pale gold | jonquiripe corn | yellow gold | old gold | amber | deep gold | amontillado sherry | deep copper | burnished | chestnutoloroso sherry | russetpeat | tawny | auburn,polished mahogany | mahogany , henna notes | burnt umber | old oak | brown sherry, | treacle

Woodford Reserve Bourbon Academy

3 Styles of Bourbon
Mature Spirits

159

WOODFORD RESERVE FLAVOR WHEEL

This flavor wheel was developed by master distiller Chris Morris.

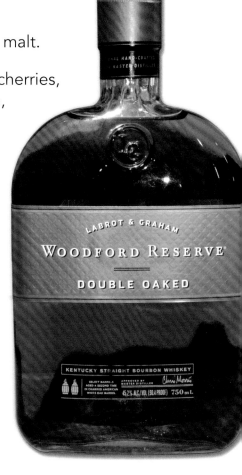

- ❖ **Sweet aromatics:** caramel, vanilla, butterscotch, maple, honey, chocolate.

- ❖ **Woods and nuts:** oak, cedar, pecan, walnut.

- ❖ **Grains:** corn, rye, wheat, malt.

- ❖ **Fruit and floral:** berries, cherries, apple, rose, honeysuckle, citrus.

- ❖ **Spices or savory:** nutmeg, coffee, tobacco, cinnamon, pepper, licorice, spearmint.

- ❖ These flavors come from the wood and grains.

- ❖ Distillers change bottle design from time to time. This is an older bottle of *Doubled Oaked*.

ALCOHOL PHYSIOLOGY

❖ A jigger (45 milliliters or 1.5 ounces) has from 105 to 140 calories from the 80–100° ethanol.

❖ Nutrition is nil.

❖ Alcohol is absorbed rapidly via the lining of the stomach and duodenum and the absorption rate depends on the rate of stomach emptying.

❖ Food (protein and fat) slows stomach emptying and absorption rate.

❖ Alcohol is oxidized in the liver by the enzyme alcohol dehydrogenase (ADH).

❖ Lower ADH activity in women means that more alcohol reaches the female bloodstream.

❖ Women have 49 percent more neurons in their olfactory lobes of the brain, making them better whiskey sensors than men.

❖ Only tiny amounts of alcohol are excreted via the lungs, urine, and sweat.

❖ The alcohol content of expired air reflects the content of the blood (breathalyzer test).

- ❖ If the liver's metabolic capacity is exceeded by consumption, blood alcohol rises and bathes the brain, resulting in intoxication.

- ❖ Heavy drinking can lead to a fatty, enlarged liver and replacement of functioning cells with connective tissue (cirrhosis), which can lead to liver failure and death.

PERSONAL OPINION

Excellent Bargain Bourbons

Buffalo Trace, Elijah Craig Small Batch, Evan Williams Single Barrel

Excellent Premium Bourbons

Blanton's, Willett Pot Still Reserve, Woodford Reserve Double Oaked,
Widow Jane

Excellent American Whiskeys

High West Campfire, Stranahan's, Yippee Ki-Yay, Rittenhouse

Representative bourbons from some major distillers in Kentucky.

DISTILLERIES

WHO OWNS WHAT?

Age International (Japan)
- Blanton's
- Ancient Age
- Rock Hill Farms

Kirin Brewing (Japan)
- Four Roses

Diageo Brands (UK)
- Bulleit
- I.W. Harper
- Forged Oak
- George Dickel
- Blade and Bow

Bacardi (Bermuda)
- Angel's Envy

Kentucky Bourbon Distillers LTD (United States)
- Willett
- Rowan's Creek
- Noah's Mill
- Johnny Drum
- Old Bardstown

Castle Brands (United States)
- Jefferson's

Beam Suntory (Japan)
- Baker's
- Basil Hayden's
- Booker's
- Knob Creek
- Jim Beam
- Maker's Mark
- Old Crow
- Old Grand Dad

Heaven Hill (United States)
- Elijah Craig
- Evan Williams
- Old Fitzgerald
- Larceny
- Henry McKenna
- Fighting Cock

Luxco (United States)
- Ezra Brooks
- Rebel Yell
- Yellowstone

Sazerac (United States)
- 1792 Ridgemont Reserve
- Very Old Barton
- Ten High
- Buffalo Trace
- Eagle Rare
- Elmer T. Lee
- Colonel E.H. Taylor Jr.
- George T. Stagg
- Pappy Van Winkle
- Weller
- Benchmark

Chatham Imports (United States)
- Michter's

Campari (Italy)
- Wild Turkey
- Russell's

Brown-Forman (United States)
- Old Forester
- Woodford Reserve
- Jack Daniel's
- Early Times

JIM BEAM

Batch

73

LEGACY

SEVEN GENERATIONS OF THE BEAM FAMILY

JACOB BEAM
1760 - 1834

DAVID BEAM
1802 - 1854

DAVID M. BEAM
1833 - 1913

COLONEL
JAMES B. BEAM
1864 - 1947

T. JEREMIAH
BEAM
1899 - 1977

BOOKER NOE
1929 - 2004

FRED NOE
1957 - PRESENT

BUFFALO TRACE

WOODFORD RESERVE

Batch 75

MAKER'S MARK

HEAVEN HILL

❖ Family-owned distillery.

❖ A devastating fire in 1996 destroyed 90,000 barrels of bourbon. Seven warehouses were destroyed in the "River of Fire." Winds of 50 miles per hour whipped flames 350 feet high.

❖ No lives or jobs were lost.

❖ Competitors Jim Beam and Brown-Forman provided production capacity and helped Heaven Hill survive for the next few years.

❖ Today, rickhouses must have a surrounding berm to contain burning whiskey.

FOUR ROSES

WILD TURKEY

BARTON'S
1792 DISTILLERY

Visit Kentucky Distilleries and
The Kentucky Bourbon Trail® Experience.

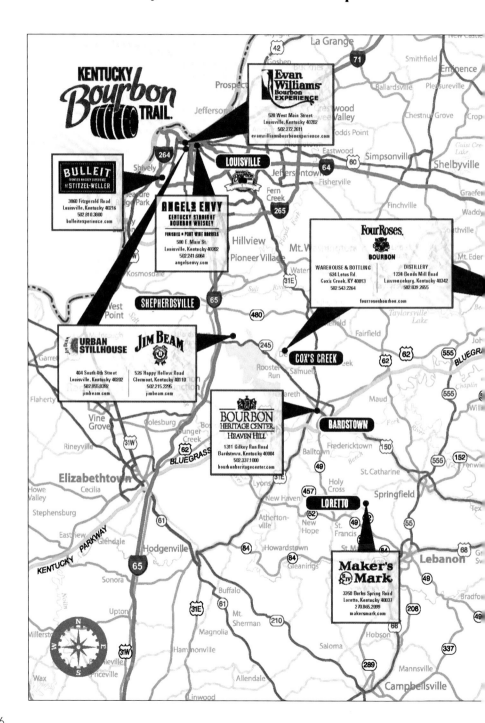

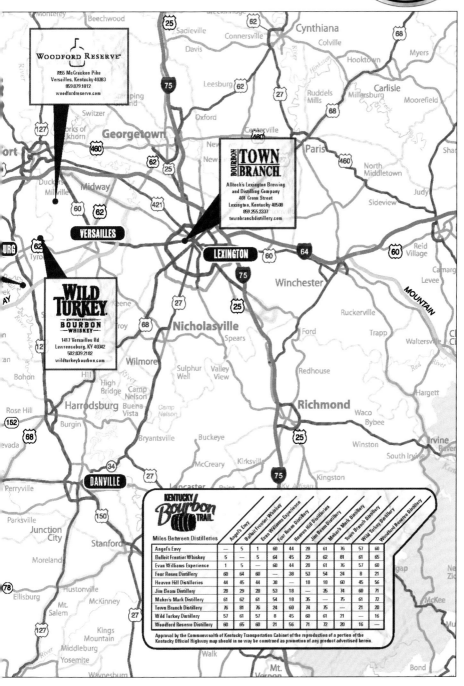

"Too much of anything is bad, but too much good whiskey is barely enough."

—Mark Twain

REFERENCES

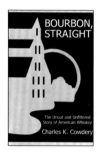

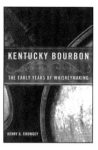

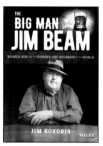
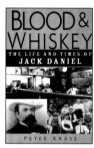

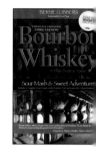

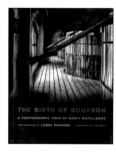
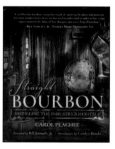
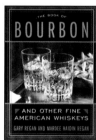

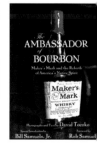

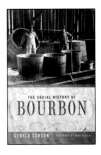

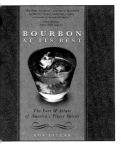

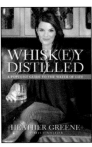

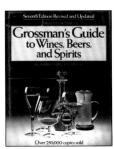

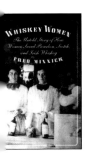

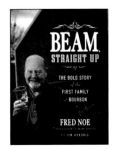

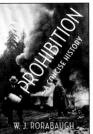

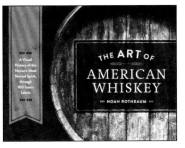

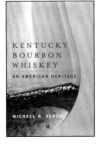

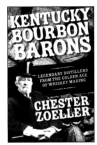

Literature Cited

Barton, Susannah Skiver. 2018. "Cracking the Aging Code." *Whisky Advocate* 27(1): 62–73.

Bryson, Lew. 2014. *Tasting Whiskey: An Insider's Guide to the Unique Pleasures of the World's Finest Spirits*. North Adams, MA: Storey Publications.

Campbell, Sally Van Winkle. 1999. *But Always Fine Bourbon: Pappy Van Winkle and the Story of Old Fitzgerald*. Louisville, KY: Limestone Lane Press.

Carlton, Carla Harris. 2017. *Barrel Strength Bourbon: The Explosive Growth of America's Whiskey*. Birmingham, AL: Clerisy Press.

Carson, Gerald. 1963 (reprint 2010). *The Social History of Bourbon*. Lexington, KY: University Press of Kentucky.

Cecil, Sam. K. 2010. *Bourbon: The Evolution of Kentucky Whiskey*. New York: Turner Publishing.

Cooper, Edward S. 2017. *John McDonald and the Whiskey Ring: From Thug to Grant's Inner Circle*. Lanham, MD: Fairleigh Dickinson University Press.

Cowdery, Charles K. 2004. *Bourbon, Straight: The Uncut and Unfiltered Story of American Whiskey*. Chicago: Made and Bottled in Kentucky.

———. 2012. *The Best Bourbon You'll Never Taste*. Chicago: Made and Bottled in Kentucky.

———. 2014. *Bourbon, Strange: Surprising Stories of American Whiskey*. Chicago: Made and Bottled in Kentucky.

Crowgey, Henry G. 1971 (reprint 2008). *Kentucky Bourbon: The Early Years of Whiskeymaking*. Lexington, KY: University Press of Kentucky.

Ewaze, Juliet O., R.C. Summerbell, and James A. Scott. 2007. "Physiological Studies of the Warehouse Staining Fungus, *Baudoinia compniacensis*." *Mycological Research III*: 1422–1430.

Getz, Oscar. 1978. *Whiskey: An American Pictorial History*. New York: David McKay.

Givens, Ron. 2008. *Bourbon at its Best: The Lore & Allure of America's Finest Spirits*. Cincinnati: Clerisy Press.

Greene, Heather. 2014. *Whisk(e)y Distilled: A Populist Guide to the Water of Life*. New York: Viking Studio.

Grossman, Harold J. and Harriet Lembeck. 1983. *Grossman's Guide to Wines, Beers, and Spirits*. 7th ed. New York: Charles Scribner's Sons.

Hogeland, William. 2006. *The Whiskey Rebellion: George Washington, Alexander Hamilton, and the Frontier Rebels Who Challenged America's Newfound Sovereignty*. New York: Scribner.

Howlett, Leon. 2015. *The Kentucky Bourbon Experience: A Visual Tour of Kentucky's Bourbon Distilleries.* Morley, MO: Acclaim Press.

Huckelbridge, Dane. 2014. *Bourbon: A History of the American Spirit.* New York: Harper Collins.

Kokoris, Jim. 2016. *The Big Man of Jim Beam: Booker Noe and the Number One Bourbon in the World.* Hoboken, NJ: Wiley.

Krass, Peter. 2004. *Blood and Whiskey: The Life and Times of Jack Daniels.* Hoboken, NJ: Wiley.

Kroll, Harry H. 1967. *Bluegrass, Belles, and Bourbon: A Pictorial History of Whiskey in Kentucky.* Cranbury, NJ: A.S. Barnes.

Lubbers, Bernie. 2015. *Bourbon Whiskey: Our Native Spirit.* Indianapolis, IN: Blue River Press.

Lucas, William F. 1970. *"Nothing Better in the Market" Brown-Forman's Century of Quality, 1870–1970.* Louisville, KY: Newcomen Society.

Minnick, Fred. 2013. *Whiskey Women: The Untold Story of How Women Saved Bourbon, Scotch, and Irish Whiskey.* Lincoln, NE: Potomac Books.

———. 2015. *Bourbon Curious: A Simple Tasting Guide for the Savvy Drinker.* Minneapolis, MN: Zenith Press.

———. 2016. *Bourbon: The Rise, Fall, and Rebirth of an American Whiskey.* Minneapolis, MN: Quarto Publishing.

Mitenbuler, Reid. 2016. *Bourbon Empire: The Past and Future of America's Whiskey.* New York: Penguin.

Noe, Fred and Jim Kokoris. 2012. *Beam Straight Up: The Bold Story of the First Family of Bourbon.* Hoboken, NJ: John Wiley and Sons.

Oliveira-Pinto, Ana V., Raquel M. Santos, Renan A. Coutinho, Lays M. Oliveira, Gláucia B. Santos, Ana T.L. Alho, Renata E.P. Leite, et al. 2014. "Sexual Dimorphism in the Human Olfactory Bulb: Females Have More Neurons and Glial Cells than Males." *PLoS ONE* 9(11): e111733. doi:10.1371/journal.pone.0111733.

Pacult, F. Paul. 2003. *American Still Life: The Jim Beam Story and the Making of the World's #1 Bourbon.* Hoboken, NJ: Wiley & Sons.

Peachee, Carol. 2015. *The Birth of Bourbon: A Photographic Tour of Early Distilleries.* Lexington, KY: University Press of Kentucky.

———. 2017. *Straight Bourbon: Distilling the Industry's Heritage.* Bloomington, IN: Indiana University Press.

Pearce, John Ed. 1970. *Nothing Better in the Market.* Louisville, KY: Brown-Forman Distillers.

Regan, Gary and Mardee Haidin Regan. 1995. *The Book of Bourbon and Other Fine American Whiskeys.* Shelburne, VT: Chapters Publishing Ltd.

Reigler, Susan. 2013. *Kentucky Bourbon Country: The Essential Travel Guide*. Lexington, KY: University Press of Kentucky.

———— and Michael Veach. 2018. *The Bourbon Tasting Notebook*. 2nd ed. Morley, MO: Acclaim Press.

Risen, Clay. 2015. *American Whiskey Bourbon and Rye: A Guide to the Nation's Favorite Spirit*. 2nd ed. New York: Sterling Epicure.

Rogers, Adam. 2014. *Proof: The Science of Booze*. Boston: Houghton Mifflin Harcourt.

Rorabaugh, W.J. 2018. *Prohibition: A Concise History*. New York: Oxford University Press.

Rothbaum, Noah. 2015. *The Art of American Whiskey: A Visual History of the Nation's Most Storied Spirit through 100 Iconic Labels*. Berkeley, CA: Ten Speed Press.

Samuels, Jr., Bill. 2000. *Maker's Mark: My Autobiography*. Louisville, KY: Butler Books.

Scott, Berkeley and Jeanine Scott. 2017. *The Kentucky Bourbon Trail*. Revised edition. Charleston, SC: Arcadia.

Scott, James A., Wendy A. Untereiner, Juliet O. Ewaze, Bess Wong, David Doyle. 2007. "*Baudoinia*, a New Genus to Accommodate *Torula Compniacensis*." *Mycologia* 99(4): 592–601.

Scott, James A., J.O. Ewaze, R.C. Summerbell, Y. Arocha-Rosete, A. Maharaj, Y. Guardiola, M. Saleh, et al. 2015. "Multilocus DNA Sequencing of the Whiskey Fungus Reveals a Continental-Scale Speciation Pattern."*Persoonia* 37: 13–20.

Spoelman, Colin and David Haskell. 2013. *The Kings County Distillery Guide to Urban Moonshining: How to Make and Drink Whiskey*. New York: Abrams.

Stewart-Howard, Stephanie. 2016. *Kentucky Bourbon & Tennessee Whiskey*. Guildfort, CT: Globe Pequot.

Toczko, David. 2012. *The Ambassador of Bourbon: Maker's Mark and the Rebirth of America's Native Spirit*. Morley, MO: Acclaim Press.

————. 2014. *Buffalo Trace: Carving the Trail to Great Bourbon*. Morley, MO: Acclaim Press.

Veach, Michael R. 2013. *Kentucky Bourbon Whiskey: An American Heritage*. Lexington, KY: University Press of Kentucky.

Wardlaw, G.M. and M. Kessel. 2002. *Perspectives in Nutrition*. 5th ed. Boston: McGraw Hill.

Young, Al. 2013. *Four Roses: The Return of a Whiskey Legend*. Louisville, KY: Butler Books.

Zoeller, Chester. 2014. *Kentucky Bourbon Barons: Legendary Distillers from the Golden Age of Whiskey Making.* Louisville, KY: Butler Books.
———. 2015. *Bourbon in Kentucky: A History of Distilleries in Kentucky.* 3rd ed. Louisville, KY: Butler Books.

Bourbon Blogs and Web Sites

https://blog.feedspot.com/
https://bottomofthebarrelbourbon.com/
http://bourbonbabe.tumblr.com/
https://www.bourbonbanter.com/
https://www.bourbonblog.com/
http://bourbonbuzz.com/
http://www.bourbondrinker.com/
http://www.bourbonenthusiast.com/
http://bourbonr.com/
https://www.bourbonsavvy.com/
http://chuckcowdery.blogspot.com/
https://www.fredminnick.com/
http://sourmashmanifesto.com/
http://www.straightbourbon.com/
https://thewhiskeywash.com/
http://www.whisky.com/
http://www.whiskeyprof.com/

Periodical

Whisky Advocate. http://whiskyadvocate.com/magazine/
A quarterly magazine for information on bourbon, Scotch, Irish, Japanese and other whiskeys.

Films about Bourbon

Made and Bottled in Kentucky: The Story of Bourbon Whiskey. 1992. Filmmaker Charles Kendrick Cowdery shows how bourbon is made, tours several Kentucky distilleries and interviews historians, and distillers.
Neat: The Story of Bourbon. 2018. Filmmaker David M. Altrogge explores the history and process of making bourbon, including its charismatic characters and best stories.

Liquor Prices in Ohio (a very useful reference point)

https://www.ohiolmp.com/brandmaster_public.php

NOTES AND FURTHER EXPLANATIONS

The vast majority of the photographs are my own. Bourbon bottles were photographed over several years as I acquired them. The photography was done either in Ohio (March to November) or in Florida (December to February). The seasonal and geographical variation of the sun's angle, cloud cover, and white vs. brown base all have an effect on the color of the bourbon in the bottle.

Batch 1 To quote from the Standards for Identity: "Whisky is an alcoholic distillate from a fermented mash of grain produced at less than 190 proof in such a manner that the distillate possesses the taste, aroma, and characteristics generally attributed to whisky, stored in oak containers (except that corn whisky need not be so stored), and bottled at not less than 80 proof, and also includes mixtures of such distillates for which no specific standards of identity are prescribed." For more than you will want to know, you can read the Standards of Identity at https://www.lawcornel.edu/cfr/text/27/5.22. (To be called whisky in Europe, three years of aging are required.) You can also find the Standards of Identity in appendix P of Grossman and Lembeck (1983). The *New York Times* (April 23, 2018) stated that worldwide, Scotch is the most popular whiskey by a large margin. The Scotch Whiskey Association reported that in 2017 85 million cases of Scotch were consumed globally vs 44 million cases of American and 28 million cases of Canadian whiskey. I like to think of bourbon and rye whiskeys as brothers while Scotch, Irish, Canadian, and Japanese whiskeys are cousins of bourbon and rye.

Batch 2 Whiskey vs. whisky is basically a distiller's spelling choice, and there are several other examples beyond those I have cited. Countries without an "e" in their name do not use an "e" in whisky. Those with an "e" in their name use an "e" in whiskey. The owners of *Maker's Mark* use "whisky" to acknowledge their Scottish ancestors. The *Maker's Mark* logo with the circle, S, IV, and star is, in fact, the "maker's mark" and is pregnant with meaning. "S" refers to the Samuels family of distillers whose original brand was T.W. Samuels; "IV" is a generational nod to the Samuels family. The current whiskey maker and chief operating officer, Rob Samuels, is the eighth-generation distiller, and his father, Bill Samuels, Jr., was the seventh. His father, Bill Samuels, was the sixth not the fourth generation of distillers (Samuels, Jr., 2000). The star represents their property (Star Hill Farms), and the broken circle symbolizes the disruption of Prohibition. The "maker's mark" concept was borrowed from pewter craftsmen who stamp their work. Likewise, the red wax seal was appropriated from cognac bottles. Be on the lookout for rare "over-dipped" (aka "slam dunked") bottles where the red wax envelopes the label. A *Maker's Mark* ad in 1995 featured an over-dipped bottle and created an overnight demand for these rare bottles (Samuels, Jr., 2000). The bottle pictured here (left, p 13) belongs to my neighbor Charlie Dlesk. Compare this over-dipped bottle to the one to its right (p 13). No two are alike since they are hand-dipped. I found this over-dipped treasure at Kroger in Mansfield, Ohio on 12 October 2018, while finalizing this book. I have been searching for years for such a bottle, and there it was, out of the blue. I asked the young clerk when it came in. He replied "It came in yesterday. I thought it was an accident and ugly, so I buried it three-deep on a bottom shelf." I thanked him. I have made repeated attempts to learn the frequency of these over-dipped bottles. Are they, say, 1/1,000, 1/10,000, 1/100,000, 1/1,000,000? Apparently, no such data are kept. When I asked this question of the *Maker's Mark* web site, I received an apologetic reply for the assumed "defect": "Thanks for reaching out to us. Unfortunately, we don't have that kind of information. It doesn't occur that often. I'm sorry that you had this issue and hope that it doesn't happen to you in the future." That naïve response evoked a smile. I wrote directly to Rob Samuels, and he graciously replied via letter: "I did wish to clarify that our bottling team members are allowed and encouraged to over hand dip a bottle whenever they are so inspired to do so." There you have it. There is apparently no way to arrive at a reliable estimate of the frequency of over-dipped bottles. Samuels, Jr., (2000) and Toczko (2012) provide further insights into *Maker's Mark*.

 If it is not made from grain, it cannot be a whiskey, but grain alone does not a whiskey make. "Spirits" are any strong, distilled, alcoholic liquor. All whiskeys are spirits, but not all spirits are whiskey.

 You must commit this page to memory.

 Don't mess with the Feds. Bourbon dumped from the barrel into a charcoal filtration system before bottling.

 I love the color of bourbon in the sunlight.

Tasseled ear of corn in Ohio field in late July. A bottle of *Old Overholt* straight rye whiskey sits on bag of rye grain. This old-time brand was once made in Pennsylvania and was the favorite of Don Draper on TV's Mad Men. This style of whiskey was called "Monongahela rye" after the river in the region where it was made (Getz 1978) and predates "bourbon" by 50 years (Pacult 2003). It survived Prohibition as "medicinal whiskey" and is now made in Kentucky by *Jim Beam*. An incentive for making whiskey in early days of America was that rum is based on sugar and the plantations were worked by slaves and owned by the British from whom we rebelled. In 1779, the Corn Patch and Cabin Rights Law took effect. Settlers who planted a corn patch (size not specified) and built a cabin (size not specified) could claim title to 400 acres of land. The distillation of liquor was an ordinary fact of life for settlers, along with making soap, tanning animal hides, and making candles (Crowgey 1971). Distilling was a wintertime activity after fall harvest and before spring planting. Crude calculations made on a cocktail napkin show that if a mule could carry four bushels of corn (about 240 pounds at 60 pounds per bushel), each bushel of which yields about 2.5 gallons of whiskey as stated by Krass (2004), then the mule could carry the equivalent of 14 bushels in the form of 35 gallons of whiskey, which would weigh about the same, assuming one gallon of whiskey weighs about seven pounds. The whiskey would be much more valuable than the same weight of corn. There are too many assumptions and unknown variables to be precise, but the point is that transporting whiskey was much more efficient than transporting grain. Pacult (2003) wrote that a packhorse could transport 4 bushels of rye or the alcoholic equivalent of 24 bushels of rye whiskey but did not explain the calculations. The notable books that deal in depth with the history of bourbon and distilling include Carson (1963), Kroll (1967), Crowgey (1971), Getz (1978), Regan and Regan (1995), Campbell (1999), Pacult (2003), Krass (2004), Cecil (2010), Veach (2013), Huckelbridge (2014), Minnick (2013, 2016), and Mitenbuler (2016). Peachee (2015) provided an elegant photographic tour of early distilleries. Spoelman and Haskell (2013) presented a concise chapter on America's whiskey history. Givens (2008) provided an excellent synopsis of each of the major distilleries. Lucas (1970) addressed the Newcomen Society in Louisville on the 100th anniversary of Brown-Forman Distillers Corporation and reviewed interesting historical anecdotes such as the first use of scented ink in newspaper ads for *Old Forester*.

Batch 8 — *Ridgemont Reserve's 1792* commemorates the year Kentucky entered the Union on June 1 as the fifteenth state. The cartoon of George Washington bottling up the Whiskey Rebellion was drawn by Walt Handelsman in 2006 for George Washington's Mount Vernon and is used with the permission of both. Getz (1978) has an especially detailed section on Washington, Hamilton, and the Whiskey Rebellion, including the reproduction of some historical documents. Hogeland (2006) literally wrote the book on the Whiskey Rebellion. After Thomas Jefferson repealed the excise tax, distilled spirits remained tax-free in the US from 1802-1862, when expenses of the Civil War necessitated its reinstitution by President Abraham Lincoln.

Batch 9 — Coat-of-arms of the French royal family Bourbon. Bourbon Street is in the French Quarter of New Orleans. New Orleans was founded over 300 years ago in 1718 and celebrated its tricentennial in 2018. As a four-year resident of New Orleans and graduate of Tulane University (MS and PhD), I know Bourbon Street. Enough said. The first advertisement for bourbon appeared on June 26, 1821, in the newspaper *Western Citizen* (Crowgey 1971). The newspaper was published in Paris, Bourbon County, Kentucky from 1808 to 1886. Crowgey (1971), Veach (2013), Cowdery (2014), and Minnick (2015) review the various explanations of the name "bourbon." Minnick (2015) mentions that the barrels were stamped "Limestone, Bourbon County, Kentucky." It is difficult to separate fact from mythology around this question.

Batch 10 *"Bound Down the River"* c. 1870. Artist unknown. Printmaker: Currier and Ives. Hand-colored lithograph. Old drawings show how barrels were transported from Kentucky to New Orleans, during which time, the bourbon obtained color and flavor from the oak. It is not inconceivable that toasting the staves in order to bend them to barrel shape resulted in some internal charring of the staves (Regan and Regan 1995). Crowgey (1971) reports that the journey from Kentucky to New Orleans took slightly over three months in 1806, during which time, a substantial portion of the whiskey cargo disappeared due to offshore trading or internal consumption. Minnick (2015) claims the voyage took a year. Regan and Regan (1995) point out that if whiskey was distilled after harvest in, say October, then shipment downstream may have needed to wait for spring floods to raise the water level. This would mean the whiskey sat in barrels until about April and then spent another two months in transport for a total of about eight to nine months of aging in the barrel. Other goods regularly transported on the flatboats included flour and tobacco.

Batch 11 The Prohibition skeleton lady is sitting on a whiskey barrel and carrying a flag that reads: "My Banner: Murder, Suicide, Despair, Poverty, Insanity, Theft, Degradation, Ignorance, Crime, Disease, No Hereafter." These are just some of the things the WCTU attributed to alcohol drinking. (Photographed at the Oscar Getz Museum of Whiskey History in Bardstown, Kentucky) *Satirical photo of a teetotaler women*, c. 1890. A century-long campaign led to Prohibition. After the Revolutionary War, whiskey was cheaper than beer, wine, coffee, tea, or milk (Rorabaugh 2018). Widespread drunkenness is said to have contributed to wife beating, child abuse, election fraud, and criminal activity. Rural fundamentalist Protestants were the strongest anti-alcohol advocates, while city-dwelling Catholics, Episcopalians, and Jews were more accepting of alcohol. Religious revivals promoted the idea that alcohol use was socially unacceptable. The Civil War slowed down the rush to Prohibition because the government needed the tax revenue from alcohol to prosecute the war. By the late 1800s and early 1900s, industrialists such as George Pullman, Thomas Edison, Henry Ford, and John D. Rockefeller opposed alcohol for the effect it had on their workforce. Leading up to Prohibition, the country was a confused and ambiguous patchwork of wet and dry states and wet and dry counties within states. The WCTU was founded in 1874 in Cleveland, Ohio, as an outgrowth of an earlier Woman's Crusade. Its most outrageous member was the ax-wielding Carrie Nation, who at nearly six feet and 175 pounds, was a formidable presence (Pacult 2003). She notoriously attacked barrels of whiskey in taverns upon instructions she claimed to have received directly from Jesus. She also hated sex, tobacco, and Teddy Roosevelt (Getz 1978). A visit to the Oscar Getz Museum in Bardstown, with its displays of Prohibitionist memorabilia helps capture the mood of the times. A similar feeling can be engendered by thumbing through Getz's book. The Anti-Saloon League, founded in Ohio in 1893, was a more moderate and effective anti-alcohol group with connections to Methodists, Baptists, and Presbyterians. The 16th Amendment to the Constitution, which allowed a federal income tax, was ratified in 1913. Dry supporters could now push for a constitutional amendment outlawing alcohol since loss of the tax on liquor could be offset by the new income tax. The major alcohol markets were in New York, Illinois, and California. Connecticut and Rhode Island were the only states to reject the 18th Amendment. The other 46 states ratified it within about a year, although legally they had seven years to do this. Without the patriotic conformity generated by WWI, the country may not have adopted Prohibition (Rorabaugh 2018).

Batch 12 If this old photo (c. 1921) makes you sad, you are indeed a whiskey lover. The man in the suit is the deputy police commissioner of New York City, John A. Leach, who is making sure confiscated whiskey is destroyed. Drugstores became de facto liquor stores during Prohibition. Charles Walgreen owned nine pharmacies in Chicago in 1916 and 525 by the end of the 1920s (Rorabaugh 2018). Minnick (2015) listed the six companies that obtained medicinal licenses. Pearce (1970) suggested that so few medicinal permits were issued because distillers did not feel it was worth the effort. Speaking of medicinal whiskey, it is, of course, a myth that whiskey is an antidote for a venomous snake bite. Nevertheless, the quip by W.C. Fields is clever: "Always carry a flagon of whiskey in case of snakebite and furthermore always carry a small snake." Prohibition nearly destroyed the distilling industry, which was given one year to sell its stock and begin another business. Many smaller distillers were consumed by the larger ones. Of the 17 distilleries making whiskey in Kentucky before Prohibition, only seven remained at repeal (Regan and Regan 1995). A loophole of home provision allowed wealthy people to stockpile a pre-Prohibition supply of alcohol for personal consumption. J.P. Morgan sequestered 1000 cases of champagne, just in case (Rorabaugh 2018). The purchase and possession of alcohol was not illegal so that prosecutors could use buyers as snitches against sellers because selling was illegal. Home use, which was legal, led to the ubiquitous cocktail party with mixed drinks that camouflaged inferior liquor.

Batch 13 Capone's police mug shot was photographed at the Oscar Getz Museum of Whiskey History. No Roaring Twenties' party was complete without whiskey. In New York City alone, in 1930, there were 625 deaths from impure alcohol, and 50,000 people in Kansas City, Oklahoma City, and Cincinnati were paralyzed. Amazingly, a Prohibition Bureau agent in Illinois deputized Ku Klux Klan members as enforcement officers. To avoid police and hijackers, bootleg drivers used souped-up six-cylinder cars such as Buicks and Studebakers to deliver their contraband. Their off-day races evolved into NASCAR (Givens 2008, Rorabaugh 2018). The "noble experiment" nickname for Prohibition is an inaccurate paraphrase of Herbert C. Hoover's words: "a great social and economic experiment, noble in motive…" (Regan and Regan 1995).

14 A "supermoon" occurs when the moon is full on the same day that it is closest to the earth, when it reaches the perigee of its elliptical orbit. I took this supermoon photograph on January 2, 2018, at 10:15 p.m. on Anna Maria Island, Florida. See Pacult (2003) and Cowdery (2014) for the interesting details of Mexican-made bourbon. Joseph L. Beam (Jim Beam's cousin) and his son Harry eventually left the Mexican operation to head up the Heaven Hill Distillery in Kentucky. Mexican bourbon was no longer an option when Congress declared bourbon to be a product of the United States in 1964. Some "moonshine" on the shelf in today's liquor stores is made from sugar, not from grain, and is therefore a rum, not a whiskey. Some "moonshine" is unaged corn whiskey. It is a clear liquid, similar to white dog. Other "moonshine" is a blend of grain and sugar-based spirits. People can make wine and beer at home for private consumption, but making your own whiskey is illegal. Spoelman and Haskell (2013) provided an excellent guide to becoming a criminal. Moonshine is so named because it was made at night to avoid detection by revenue agents, the hated tax-collectors disparagingly known as "revenuers" or "revenoors."

15 This *Chicago Daily News* headline was photographed at the Oscar Getz Museum of Whiskey History. December 5 is a day for whiskey fans to toast their favorite drink. The St. Valentine's Day massacre, organized by Al Capone, helped turn the public against Prohibition (Rorabaugh 2018). Enforcement of Prohibition was often arbitrary, corrupt, and ineffective because of too few agents for the huge job. Just as the national crisis of WWI tilted the country toward Prohibition, the Great Depression of 1929 favored repeal because it demanded more government economic services, which required greater revenue intake. The argument was made that Prohibition cost the country $1 billion a year in taxes plus $40 million each year for enforcement (Minnick 2013). Former Prohibition supporter John D. Rockefeller Jr. advocated for the repeal of prohibition and believed that the government should regulate the alcohol industry. Veterans and labor groups backed repeal. The country's mood was changing to allow more access to alcohol. To win the Democratic presidential nomination, New York Governor Franklin D. Roosevelt adopted a repeal Prohibition policy to support the economy. Roosevelt trounced Herbert Hoover in a landslide. Most states moved quickly to cancel Prohibition in order to increase tax revenue. Mississippi was the last state to end statewide prohibition in 1966, 33 years after prohibition was repealed. Prohibition had the effect of depressing per capita alcohol consumption for many decades. The statistic on dry counties is from *Louisville Business First,* December 16, 2016. The attractive *FEW* label reflects the 1893 Chicago World's Fair. Frances E. Willard, the first dean of women at Northwestern University and a dedicated feminist and suffragette, was president of the WCTU from 1879 until she died in 1898 (Rorabaugh 2018). In 2018 *Jim Beam* released a limited-edition *Repeal Batch* bourbon as a tribute to the 85th anniversary of Prohibition's repeal on 5 December 1933. You can't judge a bourbon by its price. *Jim Beam Repeal Batch* punches far above its $18 price class. Likewise, *Benchmark* is a quality bargain at $10, as is *Ancient Ancient Age 10 Star* at $15/liter.

Batch 16 Look carefully at the fine print on whiskey labels. The labeling law states that straight bourbon less than four years old must state an age, but for straight bourbon four or more years old, it is optional to state an age on the label.

Batch 17 Six-year old *Fighting Cock* is part of the trilogy of bird bourbons to appear in the 1970s, along with *Wild Turkey* and *Eagle Rare*. *Knob Creek* is nine years old. *I.W. Harper*, 15-years old, comes in an elegant decanter, an unusual bonus these days. *Barterhouse* is an "orphan barrel" whiskey, with the claim being that the barrel was lost for two decades in the historic Stitzel-Weller rickhouse and then rediscovered and bottled. The requirement for "Kentucky bourbon" was codified in 2017. Once removed from the oak barrel and bottled, maturation stops so bottled bourbon does not improve with age. However, I have noticed that age does improve with bourbon.

Batch 18 Read the label carefully to inform your decision to purchase. "Straight" is a good word to see on the label. Likewise, "Distilled and Bottled by" are also informative, because as Pappy Van Winkle was fond of saying, "Any fool with a funnel can bottle whiskey!" (Campbell 1999). Rothbaum (2015) described bourbon history via 100 historic labels. Labels on sourced whiskey that do not say Kentucky bourbon indicate there is a good probability that the bourbon was distilled at the former Seagram's distillery in Lawrenceburg, Indiana, now known as MGP (Midwest Grain Products) or colloquially as LDI (Lawrenceburg Distillers Indiana). They distill bourbon and rye whiskey for many producers who bottle and market it under their own brand name (Cowdery 2014). For example, *Bulleit, Dickel, Redemption, Templeton*, and *Willett* rye whiskeys, to name a few, all begin with the same mash bill (95 percent rye, 5 percent malted barley) at MGP. Each brand owner manipulates proof and age to differentiate their product. Some of MGP's creations are depicted by Spoelman and Haskell (2013) in family tree format. Kentucky distilleries that produce their own namesake bourbons include *1792 Barton, Buffalo Trace, Four Roses, Heaven Hill, Jim Beam, Maker's Mark, Wild Turkey,* and *Woodford Reserve* (Brown-Forman). Independent bottlers who do not do their own distilling are called non-distiller producers (NDP). This is not a pejorative term, and many of their products are excellent; it simply means they buy their whiskey from a distiller. This is sometimes the first step a brand takes before opening their own distillery. Some well-known brand names owned by NDPs include *Redemption, Jefferson's, Michter's, High West, Wathen's, Willett,* and many others. See Cowdery (2014) and Minnick (2015) for a wider discussion of this topic.

Batch 19 Some distillers publish their mash bills, but others consider their recipes to be proprietary. Don't confuse a wheated bourbon (*Weller*) with a wheat whiskey (*Bernheim*). *Weller* could be considered an affordable and younger version of *Pappy Van Winkle* since both use the same mash bill but are of different ages. I think of the 12-year-old expression of *Weller* as the incipient 15-year-old *Pappy's*. High rye bourbon was defined by Bernie Lubbers (2015, 78) in *Bourbon Whiskey*. The mash bill certainly influences the flavor of bourbon, but the amount of time and location of the barrels in the rickhouse (warehouse) also has a significant, and arguably greater, effect on taste.

Batch 20 Corn from Richland County, Ohio harvested in mid-November. Lightning photo courtesy of David FitzSimmons. Unaged corn whiskey in the United States cannot be called a whiskey in Europe or Canada because it is not aged. If a 100 percent corn mash bill is aged in new charred oak barrels, it is bourbon, not corn whiskey.

Batch 21 A pot of crushed barley grain. Diastase is a group of enzymes that catalyzes the breakdown of starch into maltose and then into glucose. Without malting (germination of barley), this enzymes group does not occur. The conversion of starch into sugar by barley's enzymes is known as saccharification. Some other single malt Scotch brands include *Ardbeg, Glenlivet, Laphroaig,* and *Macallan*. Blended Scotch may include whiskey made from various grains in addition to barley. Familiar blended brands include *Chivas, Dewar's,* and *Johnnie Walker,* the world's largest whiskey brand. *Monkey Shoulder* Scotch is a blend of malt (barley) whiskeys with no grain whiskey included. The name refers to a repetitive-stress shoulder injury of men who turned the malting barley by hand.

Batch 22 Kentucky River and limestone formation near Frankfort, Kentucky. Some distilleries cease production during the summer to conserve ground water supplies and resume in fall when the water table rises. The down time is used for maintenance.

Batch 23 This Richland County, Ohio, cornfield was photographed in late July. The corn was harvested in early November. This cooking vat (mash tank) is at *Maker's Mark*. The corn used to make bourbon is not the sweet corn people eat as corn on the cob. It is field corn (a.k.a. "dent corn") raised for cattle feed. It is harder and drier then sweet corn. Most of the corn used to make Kentucky bourbon is harvested from Kentucky and Indiana. Cooking temperatures vary with different distillers (Givens 2008). These temperatures are from Woodford Reserve Distillery (Chris Morris, personal communication); Cowdery (2014) gives different temperatures.

Batch 24 *Michter's US 1 Sour Mash* is a bit of an oddball whiskey in that it is not labeled a bourbon or rye. Its original mash bill is 50 percent corn, 38 percent rye, and 12 percent malted barley. It does not meet the 51 percent standard for either grain. In 1950, Louis Forman coined the name Michter's from the first names of his sons Michael and Peter. Cowdery (2012) reviews the complicated history of this company. Many micro distilleries use a sweet mash process. The sour mash process is generally credited to the legendary distiller of *Old Crow*, James C. Crow of the Oscar Pepper Distillery (now Woodford Reserve) about 1835, but Regan and Regan (1995) and Minnick (2016) write that the technique pre-dated Crow. His meticulous, analytical methods certainly perfected the process, and *Old Crow* was the standard by which bourbon was judged in the early days.

Batch 25 This cypress wood fermentation vat at *Woodford Reserve* holds 7,500 gallons. Note the CO_2 bubbles in the distiller's beer. In most cases, distiller's beer is around 9 percent ABV. Some yeast strains can tolerate higher alcohol content than others, but more than 18 percent ABV is lethal to even the most tolerant yeast strains. To make bourbon, the solids and liquid are kept together after cooking for fermentation and distillation. To make Scotch, the solids are filtered out after cooking, and the remaining liquid (wort) is fermented and distilled.

Batch 26 Master distiller Chris Morris carries a carboy of yeast culture and master taster Elizabeth O'Neil carries yeast subsamples at Woodford Reserve Distillery. Some distillers use dried package yeast and others culture their own specific strains. Four Roses Distillery uses two mash bills: B is 60 percent corn, 35 percent rye, and 5 percent barley, and E is 75 percent corn, 20 percent rye, and 5 percent barley. Its five yeast strains (acquired from five Kentucky distilleries when Seagram owned the label) are designated F, K, O, Q, and V. Each imparts different characteristics (F herbal, K spicy, O rich fruitiness, Q floral, and V delicate fruitiness) (Young 2013). The 10 permutations are united in *Four Roses Yellow Label*. *Four Roses Small Batch* mingles four of the recipes (B plus O 35 percent, B plus K 35 percent, E plus O 15 percent, E plus K 15 percent) from specially selected barrels. *Four Roses Single Barrel* is bottled from specially chosen barrels of the high rye mash bill B and yeast strain V. The rye used by *Four Roses* is imported from Germany whereas most bourbon distillers use rye from the northern United States and Canada.

Batch 27 This distillation equipment is at Middle West Spirits in Columbus, Ohio. Vendome Copper and Brass Works of Louisville makes gorgeous functional art in the form of stills and other apparatus for distilleries and breweries throughout the United States and the world. See Peachee (2017) for superb photographs of the copper art of Vendrome and other makers of distillery equipment. Aenaes Coffey, an Irish whiskey tax collector, perfected the continuous still in 1830; it is sometimes called a Coffey still (Bryson 2014). One of the charms of Getz's 1978 book is the reproduction of historical documents and illustrations, including a reprint of a *Scientific American* article on distillation from 1862.

Batch 28 These are two of the three pot stills at Woodford Reserve Distillery. They were made in Scotland. Pot stills are also called alembic stills. *Willett Pot Still Reserve*, arguably the most beautiful bourbon bottle, comes in 750-milliliter and 1.75-liter sizes; glass art filled with the distiller's art.

Batch 29 This small teaching still is at Distilled Spirits Epicenter's Moonshine University in Louisville, where courses about bourbons and the distilling process are taught. Barton Distillery's enormous old still in Bardstown, Kentucky, is six feet in diameter and 55 feet tall. The top third is copper and the bottom is steel. There are nine copper plates and 18 steel ones. Mash enters near the top at plate number 10.

Batch 30 *Jim Beam's* small craft distillery demonstrates the bourbon making process to visitors with a column still, low and high wine spirit safes, and a doubler. Bourbon is more than ethanol. Some congeners are retained from distillation and provide flavor, for better or worse. Here are some products of distillation that each have their own flavor and aroma in order of their boiling point: acetaldehyde, 68.4°F (20.2°C); acetone, 132.8°F (56°C); methanol, 148.6°F (64.8°C); ethyl acetate, 170.8°F (77.1°C); ethyl alcohol, 173.1°F (78.4°C); propyl alcohol, 207°F (97.2°C); water, 212°F (100°C); butyl alcohol, 243.5°F (117.5°C); acetic acid, 244.4°F (118°C); amyl alcohol, 280°F (137.8°C); and furfural, (321.8°F (161°C). The first four compounds are considered heads, the latter four are tails. Tiny amounts of some heads and tails may make it into bourbon and help form the flavor profile. You may recognize acetone as nail polish remover. Methanol (a.k.a. wood alcohol) is highly toxic and can cause blindness or death; as little as one ounce (30 milliliters) can be lethal and 100 milliliters (3.4 ounces) are typically fatal. This was a big problem with Prohibition moonshine. Acetic acid is vinegar.

Batch 31 In the spirit safe (multi-chamber tail box) at *Woodford Reserve*, density of various cuts can be measured and diverted. The other spirit safe and holding tanks are at Maker's Mark.

Batch 32 Hereford cattle feed on spent mash. A thumper does the same thing (second distillation) as a doubler, only with more noise. Low wine vapors from the beer still are sent through hot water before condensing. This produces a thumping sound as alcohol vapors bubble through the water (Reigler 2013). It is then condensed and distilled into high wine. Thumping doesn't occur in a doubler because the low wine is already liquid (Regan and Regan 1995). Barrel entry proofs are from Minnick (2015) except *Woodford Reserve*, which is from Chris Morris (personal communication). Spent mash (spent beer, slop, and stillage) is a valuable by-product of the whiskey-making process and helps distilleries recoup the cost of purchasing grain. Its food value is greater than before the distilling process (Campbell 1999). Cattle and hog raising have always been associated with whiskey distilling (Kroll 1967).

Batch 33 This white oak tree, *Quercus alba*, was photographed by Davis Sydnor of The Ohio State University Urban Forestry, before it leafed out. The photo of a white oak leaf developing fall colors is by Kathy Smith of OSU Extension/Natural Resources. The photo of white oak acorns is by Paul Wray of

Iowa State University. Tyloses are outgrowths from cells lining transport vessels and tracheids within the wood's xylem, which can expand and completely fill the lumen, thus blocking fluid movement. It is not a requirement that bourbon be aged in American white oak barrels, but practically all bourbons are. Theoretically, any oak species from any country could be used as long as it is a new charred oak container. White oak acorns are a favorite food of wild turkeys.

Batch 34 Barrel diagrams courtesy of Independent Stave Company. Brown-Forman introduced *Cooper's Craft* in 2016. It undergoes a beech and birch charcoal mellowing process not unlike the maple charcoal mellowing process of their *Jack Daniel's Tennessee Whiskey*. Before World War II, barrels held 48 gallons. War-time shortages of materials caused coopers to increase barrel size in order to use fewer barrels. The ricks in rickhouses could accommodate barrels as large as 53 gallons (200 liters) without changing the design of the ricks. A full barrel yields about 267 bottles (200 liters divided by .75 liters equals 267). Or, you could say 53 gallons divided by .2 since 750 milliliters is about one-fifth of a US gallon, hence "a fifth" of bourbon. The bilge is the bulge or fattest part of the barrel. Because of this "swelling," the surface area of a horizontal barrel in contact with the ground is reduced and therefore the barrel can pivot and be moved and directed by a single person.

Batch 35 White oak lumber dries at International Stave Company's Kentucky Cooperage in Lebanon, Kentucky, before being milled into barrel staves. This barrelhead protects very special *Colonel E.H. Taylor* bourbon in the rickhouse at Buffalo Trace. Some distilleries request a special drying regimen for their barrels. For example, *Maker's Mark* requires the staves to be air-dried outside for nine months including one summer (Samuels 2000). OFC refers to Taylor's 1870 distillery; however, the meaning of OFC is disputed. "Old Fire Copper" is the meaning according to Carson (1963), Regan and Regan (1995), Toczko (2014), Zoeller (2014, 2015) and Stewart-Howard (2016). On the other hand, "Old Fashion Copper" is used by Krass (2004) and Veach (2013). Cecil (2010) is silent on the matter, only using OFC. It probably does not mean "only for Catholics" as a tour guide suggested to me. The words "Old Fashion Copper" appear on a banner under Taylor's signature on the yellow label of *Taylor Single Barrel Bottled-in-Bond* (p 121). However, "Old Fire Copper" is shown on an old label from the George T. Stagg Distillery (Rothbaum 2015). Regan and Regan (1995) state that "Old Fire Copper" was a term applied to sweet mash to distinguish it from sour mash whiskey in the late 1800s.

Batch 36 Barrels are charred at about 284°F (140° C) at the Independent Stave Company in Lebanon, Kentucky. The barrel raising photo was provided by Independent Stave Company. Toasting occurs before charring and causes the wood starches to become sugars, which are caramelized during charring. This forms the red layer (p 103) that influences color, aroma, and flavor.

Batch 37 This alligator char barrel is on display at *Buffalo Trace*. The char levels are displayed in the rickhouse at Barton Distillery. *Jim Beam* and *Wild Turkey* specify char level #4; most distilleries use level #3 (Regan and Regan 1995), although the levels extend to #5 (Givens 2008) in rare cases.

Batch 38 These barrels are stored in the *Four Roses* single-story rickhouse. A charred barrel is fresh from the fire at International Stave Company in Lebanon, Kentucky. The rivets are from Kentucky and Missouri cooperages of International Stave Company and *Brown-Forman* cooperage.

Batch 39 Bungholes are drilled in the center of the widest stave, as shown here at the *Four Roses* rickhouse.

Batch 40 This black rickhouse is at *Maker's Mark*. Barrels are stacked six high in the single-story rickhouse at *Four Roses*. Three barrels per rick (shown at the *Bulleit* rickhouse) is the usual arrangement. Some distilleries are experimenting with palletized warehouses where barrels are stacked heads-up on pallets and can be moved around easily by forklifts to different positions.

Batch 41 The rickhouse view at *Heaven Hill* and the main aisle at *Barton's*.

Batch 42 Barrels age in the *Heaven Hill* rickhouse. The higher temperatures of summer create higher pressure inside the barrel, which facilitates movement of the bourbon into the wood and results in more rapid maturation.

Batch 43 A cross-section of a whiskey barrel stave shows the red layer where the flavor magic happens. The soak line indicates the depth of penetration of the whiskey into the oak. This sign is on display at the Jim Beam Distillery. Note the color difference in *Jim Beam Ghost* (aged one year in used oak), *Jim Beam White* (aged four years in new charred oak), and *Jim Beam Black* (aged eight years in new charred oak). All are composed of the same mash bill. Time is the artist here.

Batch 44 Barrelheads in the *Woodford Reserve* rickhouse display three pot still symbols.

Batch 45 At *Jim Beam's* nine-story rickhouse, a sign shows the arrangement of barrels and cross sectioning for mingling barrel contents from different areas of the rickhouse. The exterior wall area of floors five and six represent a special region (pink barrels) of the rickhouse, from which single barrel and small batch bottlings might be taken. Beam figures from Kokoris (2016). *Maker's Mark* will relocate some barrels to different sections of a rickhouse when necessary to achieve the taste profile. *Ten High* used to be a straight bourbon but was downgraded to a blended bourbon in 2009. The name is meant to invoke an elevated place in the rickhouse, but the bottle contains 49 percent vodka. It's a lofty name for a bottom-shelf whiskey.

 This display at the Jim Beam Distillery shows the loss of the angel's share over time. The *Pappy Van Winkle* bottle photo is courtesy of Preston Van Winkle. *Pappy Van Winkle's 23-year-old Family Reserve* at 95.6 proof is one of the most sought-after bourbons, but very few people can find this rare whiskey. List price is about $250, but the real-world price can be in the thousands, and this makes barrels and bottles attractive targets for theft as recounted by Stewart-Howard (2016). Rarity is relative, of course. If you want to search for a really rare bourbon, try finding *A.H. Hirsch 1974 16 Years Old Blue Wax*. Think $5000, but first read Charles Cowdery's *The Best Bourbon You'll Never Taste* (2012). *Angel's Envy* evokes the angel's share. Note the wings on the back of the bottle. Learn more about Pappy Van Winkle from Campbell (1999).

Batch 47 There is much more that could be stated here, but let's keep it simple.

Batch 48 A warehouse-staining fungus (a.k.a. whiskey fungus) grows on the *Wild Turkey* rickhouse and on a barrel in the *Woodford Reserve* rickhouse. This fungus is also found near very large commercial bakeries where alcohol evaporates from yeast-risen dough. For more details about *Baudoinia compniacensis*, see Scott et al. (2007) and Ewaze, Summerbell, and Scott (2007). *Baudoinia* contains five species and has a worldwide distribution (Scott et al. 2015).

Batch 49 These photos depict dumping the barrel and the bottling line at the Jim Beam Distillery. *Devil's Cut* photo by Mike Jarosick. To make *Devil's Cut*, after dumping the barrel, *Beam* coaxes the remaining whiskey from the wood of the barrel with a proprietary rinsing method (perhaps involving water, agitation, and heat) and then adds some of this liquid back to the barrel's original extra-aged contents to arrive at 90 proof. *Old Forester* is the oldest continuously produced whiskey brand in the United States, and the 1870 expression is a recreation of the first whiskey to be sold only in sealed bottles. The point of using a sealed bottle was to prevent adulteration of the contents, a common practice when whiskey was sold in jars or barrels. An 1881 ad for this whiskey, then spelled *Old Forrester*, shows three monkeys trying unsuccessfully to open a bottle (Rothbaum 2015). The implication is that no one can "monkey around" with this brand. Glass bottles became more readily available at a reasonable price with the development of hinged metal molds in the late 1860s (Regan and Regan 1995). Chill filtration consists of lowering the aged bourbon's temperature to 10–30°F (-12 to -1°C) and passing it through a silk or paper filter before bottling. Whiskey that is not chill filtered can develop a "chill haze" when cold with small flocculent remainders of esters, fatty acids, and proteins. This is not a defect; it is just chemistry, but some consumers dislike this haze for esthetic reasons. It is most apparent in whiskey below 92 proof. Some connoisseurs prefer the rich mouth feel of non-chill-filtered bourbon and also want to see the floc to be reassured that flavor has not been removed in filtration. Most bourbons are chill filtered, but some whiskeys proudly advertise the fact that they are not, including *William Larue Weller*, *George T. Stagg*, *Russell's Reserve Single Barrel*, *McKenzie*, *Jim Beam Repeal Batch* and various *High West* expressions such as *Whiskey*, *Campfire*, and *Son of Bourye*. *Stagg Jr.* is unfiltered, and *Corner Creek* is lightly filtered and comes in a colored wine-like bottle. See Minnick (2015) for more details. Used bourbon barrels are ideal for aging Scotch and Irish whiskeys because the barrel's char has been dissipated somewhat and will not overwhelm the delicate barley flavor as virgin barrels would.

Batch 50 *Booker's* is taken from the fifth floor of the nine-story rickhouse known as the "center cut" (Noe and Kokoris 2012). Kokoris (2016) describes the development of *Booker's* in detail. It is named after master distiller Booker Noe, the grandson of Jim Beam and is a high proof bourbon. A "small batch" bourbon may be from the mingling of as few as 20 barrels in the case of *Willett Pot Still* (Stewart-Howard 2016) or *Maker's Mark* to 150 barrels for Woodford Reserve to 200-400 barrels for *Knob Creek* (Givens 2008).

Batch 51 Whiskey lovers owe a debt of gratitude to Colonel Edmund H. Taylor, Treasury Secretary John G. Carlisle, and President Grover Cleveland for protecting the whiskey-drinking public. The Bottled-in-Bond Act specifies the standards under which the whiskey was made. Although considered a badge of honor by some, B-I-B in today's market does not mean it is superior to other whiskeys or that you will prefer it to non-B-I-B products. Nevertheless, it's an informative piece of data to find on a whiskey label, as is the word "straight." Edmund H. Taylor Jr. was the grandnephew of 12th president, Zachary Taylor. John Carlisle was a representative, senator, and then secretary of the treasury from Kentucky. He is responsible for the "Carlisle allowance," which prevents the federal government from taxing the angel's share. Carlisle's image is engraved on the bottled-in-bond strip that covers the cork of Taylor's B-I-B bourbon. The bonded warehouse was a response to the Whiskey Ring Scandal of the Ulysses S. Grant administration, exposed in 1875, whereby a group of distillers and government officials in St. Louis, Milwaukee, and Chicago conspired to circumvent federal taxes on whiskey. The public became incensed that stolen tax money was used to support Grant's re-election in 1872. Treasury Secretary Benjamin H. Bistow launched a secret probe that resulted in 110 convictions, including Grant's army buddy, John McDonald, the Internal Revenue supervisor in St. Louis. Grant's secretary, Orville E. Babcock, was indicted but acquitted due to Grant's testimony. Three million tax dollars were recovered. See Carson (1963) for all the intriguing and salacious details. Cooper (2017) produced a book-length exposé. The three offending cities all became important beer producing centers.

Batch 52 President William Howard Taft deserves credit for making a decision that was very unpopular among the rectifiers who sold "imitation" (blended) whiskey. *Russell's* is named for *Wild Turkey's* master distiller, Jimmy Russell.

Batch 53 The nearly infinite diversity of tastes in bourbons is staggering when one considers the possible permutations in this short list of seven influences. The distiller Basil Hayden's is, in fact, the person honored in *Old Grand Dad*. Both are *Beam* brands. *Baker's* is named after Baker Beam, the grandnephew of Jim Beam (Kokoris 2016) and is aged for seven years. *Basil Hayden's*, *Baker's*, *Knob Creek*, and *Booker's* form the *Jim Beam* small batch collection of premium brands introduced in 1992. Each has a different flavor profile and proof. Elmer T. Lee was the distiller at George T. Stagg Distillery who created *Blanton's*. *Noah's Mill* is a high proof blend of bourbons from *Willett*. *Town Branch* is a new brand established in 2011 by Alltech of Lexington, Kentucky. *Larceny* and *Rebel Yell* are wheated bourbons.

Batch 54 Many thanks to Bernie Lubbers for allowing me to use his excellent diagram that appeared in his book *Bourbon Whiskey: Our Native Spirit* (Blue River Press, 2015). Regan and Regan (1995) provided interesting step-by-step directions and a recipe for making 988 gallons of 90-proof, five-year-old bourbon.

Batch 55 Gunpowder/proof test: For this photograph, my neighbor and bourbon-sipping buddy, Charlie Dlesk, and I used one-eighth teaspoon (one gram) of black gunpowder and 10 drops (0.2 milliliter) of whiskey (*Wild Turkey 101*) delivered from a disposable eyedropper pipette into a spoon and a BBQ flame starter to achieve ignition. My Nikon D300 was set on continuous high-speed shutter release at six frames per second. Kids, don't try this at home. Do not confuse temperature and proof. The symbol used is the same. Crowgey (1971) discussed spirits as "bearing Proof of Gunpowder." Rogers (2014) discussed the concept of "proof" in book-length format.

Batch 56 One-inch diameter holes were drilled four inches apart (center to center) in a barrel stave so *Blanton's* stoppers could be positioned along its length in a race sequence from start (stopper B) to finish (stopper S). Note the position of the jockey's head and hands and the horse's legs. This bourbon was created by Elmer T. Lee, who was trained by Albert B. Blanton, at the George T. Stagg Distillery (which became Buffalo Trace). Buffalo Trace Distillery also produces a bourbon named for Lee. *Old Forester President's Choice* was actually the first single barrel bourbon issued in the 1930s, but it was discontinued in 1971 (Chris Morris, personal communication). It was available to a limited number of aficionados. *Blanton's* is the first post-Prohibition, generally available, single-barrel bourbon. One barrel yields about 240 bottles of *Blanton's* (Regan and Regan 1995).

The answer to this question is not worth a bar fight, and I think it is a distinction without a difference. During the Lincoln County Process (LCP), the basic high pH of the sugar maple interacts with the acidic low pH of the alcohol, resulting in a reduction in acidity which our mouth interprets as mellowing. The pure carbon charcoal dust also removes or reduces some congeners and oils. Nothing is added to the spirit, but LCP alters and removes some character (Chris Morris, personal communication). The changes are reductive, not additive. The federal government's Standard of Identity does not include Tennessee Whiskey as a category (Bryson 2014), and Tennessee Whiskey meets the legal standards of a straight bourbon (Cowdery 2014, 36), although Cowdery (2004, 122) alludes to a letter from the Treasury Department stating that Tennessee Whiskey is distinct from bourbon because the LCP is not used on bourbon made outside Tennessee. Krass (2004, 224) cites the same 1941 letter. Minnick (2015) reviews this in more detail. The distinction between bourbon and Tennessee Whiskey is a State of Tennessee designation and not a federal law. Some distillery people are reluctant to say a whiskey that undergoes LCP is a bourbon since the flavor is altered (Noe and Kokoris 2012). On the other hand, the North American Free Trade Agreement defines Tennessee Whiskey as "straight bourbon whiskey authorized to be produced only in the State of Tennessee" (Minnick 2015). Does Tennessee Whiskey mean whiskey made in Tennessee or whiskey that has undergone the Lincoln County Process? The 2013 state law just confuses the issue by defining the two things as identical yet allowing an exception for *Prichard's*. Due to the redrawing of Lincoln County boundaries, the Jack Daniel's Distillery is in Moore County, and the George Dickel Distillery is in Coffee County about 12 miles away. *George Dickel* has a very high corn content of 84 percent with eight percent each of rye and barley (Risen 2015), and, unlike *Jack Daniels*, *Dickel* is chill filtered before it is charcoal-mellowed (Stewart-Howard 2016).

Read the label carefully.

It looks like bourbon, taste like bourbon, and smells like bourbon, but *Crown Royal's Bourbon Mash* is Canadian whiskey. *Crown Royal* is the largest selling Canadian whiskey in the United States and was acquired by *Diageo* when it purchased the *Seagram's* portfolio in 2000.

Seagram's 7 cannot be called a whiskey in Europe because of the high distillation proof of the grain neutral spirits. Blended whiskey in the United States must not fall below 80 proof.

The black bottle was intended to stand out and be recognized on the bar shelf. The tree on the bottle is a buckeye. Go bucks! During proof corrections for this book, Middle West Spirits discontinued the black bottle and replaced both the bottle and its contents with an "improved" version of the whiskey's flavor profile. It is now in a clear bottle labeled Straight Wheated Bourbon Whiskey and is 95 proof instead of the original 90 proof. The name *Oyo* is not used. Both the old and new whiskeys are called Michelone Reserve in homage to the grandfather who was its inspiration. It is a true four-grain bourbon with a mash bill of 65% corn, 17% wheat, 13% rye, and 5% barley cooked together. The final 3% of the barley is added at the end of cooking. The copper-trimmed label bears no age statement. Other four-grain straight bourbons are produced by craft distilleries in upstate New York. *Black Button* Distillery of Rochester, NY uses a mash bill of 60% corn, 20% wheat, 9% rye and 11% barley. The corn is cooked at 195°F, wheat and rye are cooked at 155°F. The mash is cooled to 135°F and the barley is added. No setback is used so it is a sweet mash process. The bourbon is aged for two years in 23 or 30-gallon new barrels charred to level 3.5. *Iron Smoke* Distillery of Fairport, NY produces a four-grain straight bourbon and uses apple wood smoked wheat in its mash bill. It is aged for two years in #3 charred new oak barrels. Pacult (2003) mentioned that rye and wheat "are not considered complementary grains by distillers for the creation of whiskey." I see no reason for this statement and, in my limited experience, four-grain bourbons and whiskeys can be quite tasty. Another way to make a four-grain straight bourbon is to blend straight wheated bourbon with straight ryed bourbon as is done by *Blood Oath* (Pact No. 1, 2015 and Pact No. 2, 2016). They cleverly set the proof to human body temperature, 98.6°, and package the bottle in a coffin-like wooden box. Perhaps they are trying to stake out the vampire market?

Batch 63 Now is a great time for whiskey lovers as small craft artisanal distilleries are getting very creative. In addition to Hillrock Estates of Hudson Valley, NY and Chattanooga Whisky Company, *Blade and Bow* produces a straight bourbon by the solera aging process which uses some of the last remaining bourbon from the noteworthy Stitzel-Weller Distillery of Shively, KY. The five-key logo of *Blade and Bow* symbolizes the five keys of bourbon production: grains, yeast, fermentation, distillation, and aging. The *blade* is the shaft of a key and the *bow* is the handle that turns the key. The five keys are numbered and collectible. A ring of five heavy brass keys served as a door knocker at the Stitzel-Weller Distillery (Campbell, 1999).

Batch 64 Flavored bourbons are better classified as liqueurs (alcoholic beverages made by mixing spirits with flavoring) rather than whiskeys (Grossman and Lembeck 1983). *Wild Turkey's American Honey* set the stage for this trend in 1976. *Red Stagg* by Jim Beam is another very popular expression. Either maple or pecan bourbon over melting vanilla ice cream is a gustatory orgasm. Believe it or not, there is even a kosher Kentucky straight bourbon. It is *Old Williamsburg. Oy vey!* Read about it in Regan and Regan (1995). I am assuming it is not a favorite of Risen (2015) who writes, "*Old Williamsburg* is the *Manischewitz* of bourbon." On the other hand, *Widow Jane* is labeled kosher and is a personal favorite.

Batch 65 The barrel with extra staves of French oak was photographed at Maker's Mark Distillery. Small craft distilleries and the surging bourbon renaissance are pushing the big boys to more creative and possibly better expressions. Buffalo Trace Distillery in collaboration with Last Drop (a family-run rare-spirits company) is experimenting in the opposite direction. They are trying to slow aging by storing barrels in a refrigerated rickhouse. By keeping Rickhouse P at a constant 45°F (7.2°C), they expect the bourbon will age very slowly and retain more fruit flavors while avoiding the excessively woody taste of over-aged bourbon. The plan is to keep these barrels slowly aging for 35-50 years. It is a gamble, and the results may not be known until around the year 2068. See the *New York Times* of 29 Oct. 2018 for more details.

Batch 66 Whiskey for very impatient people. Marketplace response will determine if these non-traditional processes survive the test of time, pun intended. Barton (2018) reviewed the tech-aged processes.

Batch 67 A shot glass does not have enough air space to allow aroma to vaporize and accumulate so the bourbon can be "nosed." Symbolically and functionally, the Glencairn glass is shaped like a Scottish thistle. The bulbous bowl maximizes the interface of whiskey and air and facilitates nosing. The glass was first made in 2001.

Batch 68 The color bar from the *Whisky Magazine* blog: http://www.whiskymag.com/nosing_course/part3.php. Organizing a bourbon tasting at home with your friends is fun. But eat dinner first and avoid spicy foods that linger on the palate. Remember, there is no correct answer to what you must taste in bourbon. Every person's senses are unique. But you do get more perceptive with experience. A flight is a grouping of three or more samples arranged to demonstrate differences and similarities in proof, mash bills, age, etc. Between samples, eat bland crackers and sip water. The first bourbon in a flight is often at a disadvantage so in a blind tasting, slip it in again and see how it fares compared to the first serving.

Batch 69 The flavor wheel for *Woodford Reserve Double Oaked*, courtesy of Chris Morris, is an example of what could be done for every bourbon, and each would be different. Don't worry if you can't identify all these flavors. No one can, and it takes years of experience to learn to identify a few of them. When you first taste butterscotch or vanilla or cinnamon in a bourbon, you will remember it as an "aha" moment. Greene (2014) does an especially good job with the difficult task of describing the aromas and tastes of whiskey. Reading her will help you form your own descriptions. Compare this older bottle of *Double Oaked* with the new one depicted earlier on p 152. Other noticeable bottle changes involve *Elijah Craig's 12-year-old Small Batch* (p 164), which no longer says "12 years old" in big red numerals, and *Jim Beam's Black Double Aged 8 Years* (p 103) now says *Extra Aged*, but no longer claims eight years.

Batch 70 A jigger is the standard shot of whiskey and is equal to 1.5 ounces, 45 milliliters, or three tablespoons. If you want more technical information on alcohol physiology, consult Wardlaw and Kessel (2002). A postmortem study of female and male brains indicated there is a pronounced sex-related difference in the absolute number of total, neuronal and non-neuronal cells in the olfactory bulbs, favoring women 40 percent to 50 percent, even when corrected for mass. For further details, see Oliveira-Pinto et al. (2014). This is likely why most tasting panels in distilleries have historically been female. Thanks to Susan Reigler for that insight. For more about women in whiskey, see Minnick (2013). Helpful whiskey books authored by women include Carlton (2017), Stewart-Howard (2016), Greene (2014), and Reigler (2013), Reigler and Veach (2018). Female-authored books about the bourbon industry include Campbell (1999) and Peachee (2015, 2017).

71 You can't go wrong with any of these, but *your* favorites are *yours* to decide. A frequently asked question is, "What is your favorite bourbon?" An honest answer requires too many qualifications to be a simple answer. I agree with everything said by Carlton (2017, 161) in her full-page response. Read it. *Elijah Craig* no longer claims a 12-year age statement. *Widow Jane* is sourced 10-year old Kentucky bourbon brought to proof by the addition of mineral-rich limestone water from a mine in upstate New York. *High West Campfire* is a ménage à trois of straight rye, straight bourbon, and peaty, blended malt Scotch. The latter imparts a smokiness befitting the name "campfire." Since *Stranahan's Colorado Whiskey* is made by a sweet mash process, no two batches are the same. *Yippee Ki-Yay* is a blend of straight rye whiskeys finished in vermouth and syrah barrels by High West. The name is an old cowboy exclamation of joy that was appropriated by Bruce Willis in the 1988 movie, *Die Hard*. Google the movie for the complete context. I discovered *Basil Hayden's Dark Rye* too late to add it to the photograph, but it deserves to be among this group. After sipping a bourbon that's new to you, write down your impressions and compare notes with Cowdery (2004), Minnick (2015), and the creative writing of Risen (2015) and Reigler and Veach (2018).

72 I found this very revealing and a little scary. The "American spirit" has a lot of foreign ownership. Obviously, I can't list all bourbons on two pages, but the major players are here. See Spoelman and Haskell (2013) for a family tree of bourbon brands. Age International products are made at Buffalo Trace Distillery but are not owned by Sazerac. Likewise, Van Winkle products are family owned but made at Buffalo Trace. Diageo is the world's largest alcoholic drinks company; the empire includes major brands of Scotch, rum, vodka, gin, bourbon, etc. Only four companies (Brown-Forman, Beam Suntory, Sazerac, and Heaven Hill, in that order) produce most of the bourbon sold today.

73 The Jim Beam Distillery offers one of the most extensive tours in the business and is an excellent place for a novice to begin a deeper understanding of what goes on in a distillery. The Beam family has been involved in whiskey making since 1795. "Beam" is the English spelling of the German "Boehm". A comprehensive review of the Beam family and its contribution to bourbon distilling is provided by Pacult (2003) and augmented by Noe and Kokoris

(2012) and Kokoris (2016). Regan and Regan (1995) present a concise summary of the Beam family as did Carlton (2017), who includes a family tree. *Jim Beam White Label* is the best-selling bourbon in the world. Crowgey (1971) reviewed the first 50 years of whiskey making in Kentucky and pointed out that many written statements about bourbon's background have "inadequate or nonexistent factual bases." Consult Cowdery (2014) and Minnick (2015) for fascinating expositions of the creation myths and backstories of various major bourbon brands.

Batch 74 Barrels can be seen in the windows of the brick rickhouse. Buffalo Trace is named for the pathways created by migrating bison where they crossed the Kentucky River in the 18th century. Whiskey has been distilled here since 1787. Toczko (2014) provides a stunning pictorial tribute to the Buffalo Trace Distillery including photographic portraits of E.H. Taylor, Jr. (1830-1923), George T.Stagg (1835-1893), and Albert B. Blanton (1881-1959).

Batch 75 A barrel run is pictured in front of one of the many limestone buildings on the Woodford Reserve campus. The second photo captures detail of shutters on the limestone rickhouse built in 1890. The distillery is a National Historic Landmark and has the only stone rickhouse in use today. Distillation on this site began in 1812.

Batch 76 A small section of a 37-by-6-foot glass ceiling in a *Maker's Mark* rickhouse was made by artist Dale Chihuly. *Maker's Mark* is one of the most beautiful distillery campuses and is designated a National Historic Landmark. Distillation on this site began in 1805. The Samuels family acquired it in 1953. Samuels (2000) and Toczko (2012) illustrate the history of the brand.

Batch 77 *Heaven Hill* is named after William Heavenhill, a distiller born in 1783. Heaven Hill Distillery, a family-owned company, produced its first whiskey in 1935, after Prohibition. After the 1996 fire, distillery operations were moved to Louisville when the family purchased the old Bernheim Distillery in 1999. The visitor's center and some 40-odd rickhouses, holding at least 900,000 gallons of maturing whiskey, are located in Bardstown. A *Heaven Hill* press release dated November 4, 2016, put the 1996 fire loss at over 90,000 barrels of bourbon. Cecil (2010) indicates it was about 105,000 barrels, but most importantly, their yeast was not lost (Givens 2008).

Batch 78 *Four Roses* has two campuses about an hour's drive apart. The unique one-story rickhouses and bottling facility can be seen at Cox's Creek, and the distillery, with its 1910 Spanish mission-style architecture, is located near Lawrenceburg, Kentucky. The latter has earned a place on the National Register of Historic Places. *Four Roses* was formerly owned by *Seagram's* and sold to Kirin Brewing of Japan in 2001 when *Seagram's* folded. Young (2013) recounts the history of the brand.

The Wild Turkey Distilling Company produced its first whiskey in 1869. The patio outside the tasting room has a beautiful view of the Kentucky River and highway and railway bridges. Kids of all ages enjoy riding the Wild Turkey.

Open-air fermentation tanks dissipate heat generated during fermentation. The stillhouse and other buildings of the Barton 1792 Distillery have the look, feel, and functionality of an industrial complex due to the age of the buildings, many of which date from about 1944. *Tom Moore Bourbon* was made on this site in 1879 and the eponymous spring-fed water supply acknowledges this heritage.

81

I highly recommend a driving vacation through the Kentucky Bourbon Trail® area. I suggest multiple three-day visits over several years rather than trying to do it all at once. Make Bardstown your base camp and each day explore in a different direction until you've seen it all from Louisville to Lexington. Download the map from: http://10vsslmt3js29lu005tjzl1e.wpengine.netdna-cdn.com/wp-content/uploads/2013/01/map_brochure_web.pdf. Don't forget to include *Barton's* (Bardstown), Independent Stave Company (Lebanon), and *Buffalo Trace* (Frankfort), which are *not* part of the Kentucky Distiller's Association (KDA). The Kentucky Bourbon Trail® area is the KDA's designated trademark, and I appreciate their permission to reproduce their map. *Barton's* and *Buffalo Trace* (both owned by Sazerac) are in the region and worth visiting. Independent Stave Company is one of the most interesting places you will visit. In preparation, you must read Susan Reigler's *Kentucky Bourbon Country: The Essential Travel Guide* (2013). Scott and Scott (2017) is also a helpful reference to the distilleries located in this area. Stewart-Howard (2016) provided recent synopses of the major distilleries located in Kentucky and Tennessee. For stunning photographs of Kentucky distilleries and their equipment, see Howlett (2015) and Peachee (2015, 2017).

82

My glass menagerie was photographed in my home library by my friend Terri Fisher. Books and bourbon are two of my favorite things. To combine them is exquisite. Now if I can only figure out a way to include fish. I suppose I could say something about "drinking like a fish", but that would be too cheesy. Actually, only marine bony fish "drink like a fish". Their body fluids are less salty than their environment. Therefore, water flows out of the fish via osmosis. To prevent dehydration, they constantly drink sea water and excrete the extra salt via specialize cells on the gills and through the gut. Freshwater fish, on the other hand, are saltier than their environment. Water diffuses into their body via oral and gill membranes. They must excrete copious quantities of very dilute urine to keep in osmotic balance. Chloride cells on gills actively transport salt into the fish to replace what is lost in urine. Sharks evolved a third path by retaining high concentrations of urea in their tissue fluids and are in osmotic equilibrium with their environment. So there! No extra charge for such interesting information in a bourbon book. Natives of New Orleans and Bourbon St. would know this as a lagniappe (pronounced lan-yap meaning "a little something extra"). Salute!

Batch 83 Bourbon books are like bourbon; each one has something slightly different to offer. These are the whiskey books I purchased and read as part of my preparation to write this book. Every one of them is worth reading! If you can only read one, a good place to start is Regan and Regan (1995) even though it is nearly 25 years old. It has an excellent general bourbon history section as well as concise brand histories of many prominent labels but be aware that some brand information is out of date.

ACKNOWLEDGMENTS

I would like to thank Teri Smith of Independent Stave Company for permission to photograph charring of the barrels at the Kentucky Cooperage and for supplying the barrel diagrams and photograph of the barrel raising. Philip and Connie Prichard made it possible for me to photograph *Prichard's Tennessee Whiskey*. Preston Van Winkle provided the photo of *Pappy Van Winkle 23-Year-Old* since I am highly unlikely to ever find, much less afford, my own bottle. Patrick Hicks of Hurricane Hank's Liquors, Holmes Beach, Florida, allowed me to photograph the jar of moonshine. Kathy Smith, program director for forestry at The Ohio State University Extension School of Environment and Natural Resources, located the white oak and leaf photos, and Paul Wray of Iowa State University allowed me to use his white oak acorn photograph.

My neighbor, drinking buddy, and honorary much older brother, Charlie Dlesk, served as the pyromaniac for the gunpowder test photo. Another neighbor, Bob Mowry, allowed me to photograph his cows and corn field. The photographs of the corn-on-the-cob, rye and barley grain were taken at Elzy Milling in Bellville, Ohio. My former student and bourbon sipping buddy, Michael Jarosick, DO, photographed the *Devil's Cut* bottle and reviewed an early draft of the manuscript. David FitzSimmons, PhD, generously allowed me to use his lightning photograph.

Ryan Lang and Josh Daily of Middle West Spirits in Columbus, Ohio, allowed me to photograph their beautiful back bar and explained the details of their four-grain bourbon. Heather Allen, PhD, OSU professor of chemistry, helped me think about molecular movement of water and ethanol through barrels.

Bernie Lubbers, Heaven Hill's American whiskey brand ambassador and renowned "whiskey professor," graciously critiqued the manuscript and offered many helpful suggestions. He also kindly permitted the use of his bourbon-making summary diagram. Susan Reigler, noted bourbon and travel writer whose two immensely useful books are cited in the references, made several helpful suggestions for improvement in content. Chris Morris, master distiller at Woodford Reserve, reviewed the manuscript and provided many suggestions that make me seem knowledgeable. Chris also generously granted me permission to use his flavor wheel.

Rob Allanson, *Whisky Magazine* editor, made multiple efforts to locate the bourbon color bar on my behalf.

Max Wolfram, PhD, read the entire manuscript and pointed out inconsistencies and unclear statements for correction. Thanks to artist Walt Handelsman and Dawn Bonner, manager of visual resources at George Washington's Mount Vernon, for permission to use Walt's brilliant cartoon of George Washington bottling up the Whiskey Rebellion. Examine it closely for clues to its meaning. I appreciate the Kentucky Distiller's Association permission to reproduce their Kentucky Bourbon Trail® map.

I appreciate the confidence in my manuscript continually expressed by Acclaim Press publisher Douglas Sikes from our first contact, and I am grateful to managing editor Randy Baumgardner and his design team for translating my vision of the book into a reality that exceeded my expectations. As always, I am grateful to my wife, Rita, who insulates me from dealing with the real world while I read and write books.

ABOUT THE AUTHOR

Tim M. Berra received a PhD in biology from Tulane University and is academy professor and professor emeritus of evolution, ecology, and organismal biology at The Ohio State University.

He is a three-time recipient of Fulbright Fellowships to Australia and the author of eight books and more than 85 scientific papers.

He holds concurrent positions as a university professorial fellow at Charles Darwin University and research associate at the Museum and Art Gallery of the Northern Territory, Darwin, Australia.

He is an executive bourbon steward and a member of the Stave & Thief Society. Tim currently has about 150 whiskeys in his glass menagerie.

Tim has published eight previous books: *William Beebe: An Annotated Bibliography* (1977), *An Atlas of Distribution of the Freshwater Fish Families of the World* (1981), *Evolution and the Myth of Creationism: A Basic Guide to the Facts in the Evolution Debate* (1990), *A Natural History of Australia* (1998), *Freshwater Fish Distribution* (2001), *2nd edition* (2007), *Charles Darwin: The Concise Story of an Extraordinary Man* (2009), and *Darwin and His Children: His Other Legacy* (2013).

Tim and his wife of 52 years, Rita, live on a 20-acre wooded property in Amish country near Bellville, Ohio. They are surrounded by a library of over 5,000 books, a stream with 44 species of fishes, and a lake.

The Stave & Thief Society Bourbon Certification Program is the official bourbon education course of the Kentucky Distiller's Association. This program was created by the Distiller Spirits Epicenter in 2015 via its Moonshine University with input from an advisory panel of distilling experts including Master Distillers and educators. Certification establishes a standard platform of non-branded, fact-based education in bourbon with a focus on production and sensory analysis. There are two levels: Certified Bourbon Steward is achieved by self-study of the Society's Handbook and passage of an on-line test; Executive Bourbon Steward involves course work in the classroom, distillery, and laboratory at Distilled Spirits Epicenter in Louisville and passage of an examination. Details can be found at https://staveandthief. com/. The meaning of the Roman numerals on the Society's medallion are:

- CXXV = 125. Bourbon cannot be barreled higher than 125 proof.
- LI = 51. Bourbon mash bill must be at least 51% corn.
- CLX = 160. Bourbon cannot be distilled higher than 160 proof.
- I = 1. Bourbon barrels may be used only once.
- MDCCLXXVI = 1776. American Independence. Bourbon is a product of the United State of America.

Index

Numerical

19 Crimes The Banished 14
1792 Ridgemont Reserve 27, 169, 202
1800 Silver 15

A

additives 16
Age International 168, 214
age requirement 44
A.H. Hirsch 1974 16 Years Old Blue Wax 208
Alcohol and Tobacco Tax and Trade Bureau (TTB) 18
alcohol dehydrogenase 162
alcohol physiology 162
aldehydes 72
Allanson, Rob 219
Allen, Heather 218
Amendment to the Constitution
  16th 200
  18th 32, 34, 36, 200
  21st 40
American Born Moonshine 39
Ancient Age 168
Ancient Ancient Age 49
Angel's Envy 109, 150, 151, 168, 208
angel's share 108, 208
Anna Maria Island, Florida 201
Anti-Saloon League 200
Ardbeg 10, 203
azeotropic 70

B

Babcock, Orville E. 209
Bacardi 168
backset 60
Baker's 126, 168, 210
Bardstown, KY 94
barley 50, 54, 58, 147, 202, 203, 204, 211, 212
barrel
  charring 30, 78, 87, 102, 199, 206
  making 82, 84, 86
  rivets 90, 207
  staves 82, 86, 206
  toasting 87, 199, 206
barrel entry proof 76, 77, 205
barrel strength bourbon 118

Barterhouse 46, 202
Barton's 1792 Distillery 184, 207, 216
Basil Hayden's 50, 127, 168, 210
Basil Hayden's Dark Rye 214
Beam, Baker 210
Beam, Colonel James B. 171
Beam, David 171
Beam, David M. 171
Beam, Harry 201
Beam, Jacob 171
Beam, Jim 209, 210
Beam, Joseph L. 38, 201
Beam, T. Jermiah 171
Beam Suntory 168, 214
Benchmark 169, 202
Bernheim Distillery 215
Bernheim Original 50, 51, 202
Berra, Louis H. 3
Berra, Yogi 3
Big House 123
bilge 82, 206
Bistow, Benjamin H. 209
Black Button 147, 212
Blade and Bow 148, 168, 212
Blanton, Albert B. 210, 215
Blanton's 134, 135, 164, 168, 210
Blended American Whiskey 144
Blood Oath 212
Bonner, Dawn 219
Booker's 118, 168, 209, 210
Bottled-in-Bond Act 1897 118, 120, 209
bottling 114, 115, 116, 208, 215
Bound Down the River 199
bourbon
  aging 30, 44, 46
  blended 144, 146
  definition 16
  finished 150
  flavored 150, 212
  flavor wheel 161
  high rye 203
  history 23
  kosher 212
  making summary 126
  Mexican-made 201
  name 28
  straight 44, 147, 148, 150, 211
  tasting 158
  wheated 202, 210
Bourbon County, Kentucky 28, 199
Bourbon royal family 28, 198
Bourbon Street 28, 198
Bourbon Whiskey 203
brand names and ownership 168, 169
brandy 14
Brown-Forman 78, 82, 96, 169, 178, 198, 202, 206, 207, 214
Buffalo Trace 77, 96, 134, 164, 166, 169, 202, 207, 216
Buffalo Trace Distillery 172, 210, 212, 214, 215
Bulleit 10, 50, 168, 202, 207
bung 92

C

Campari 169
Canadian whiskey 10, 38, 142, 196, 211

Capone, Al 37, 200, 201
Carlisle, John G. 120, 209
Castle Brands 168
Chacho 154
char level 88, 89, 147, 207
Chatham Imports 169
Chattanooga Whiskey 149
Chattanooga Whiskey Experimental Distillery 148
Chattanooga Whisky Company 212
Chicago Daily News 201
Chihuly, Dale 215
chill filtration 208
chill haze 208
Chivas 203
cirrhosis 163
Civil War 198, 199
Cleveland, Grover 120, 209
Cleveland Whiskey 155
Coffey, Aenaes 204
cognac 14, 29, 112
Colonel E.H. Taylor Jr. 121, 169, 206
Columbus, Ohio 146, 204, 218
congeners 72, 108, 136, 154, 205, 211
cooking 58, 203, 204
cooper 82
cooper, cooperage 82
Cooper's Craft 83, 206
copper 42, 72, 204, 205
corn 16, 24, 50, 52, 54, 58, 147, 160, 197, 198, 201, 203, 204, 211, 212, 221
Corner Creek 48, 209
Corn Patch and Cabin Rights Law 198
Cox Creek, KY 114
craft distillers 68, 155
Crow, James C. 204
Crown Royal 11, 142, 211
Crown Royal Bourbon Mash 143, 211
croze 90

D

Daily, Josh 218
Devil's Cut 208, 218
Dewar's 203
Diageo 168, 211
diastase 203
Dickel 202
distillation 66, 70, 72, 76, 204, 205, 212, 215
Distilled Spirits Epicenter 205, 221
distiller's beer 62, 66, 72, 76, 204
Dlesk, Charlie 197, 210, 218
doubler 72, 75, 76, 205
Draper, Don 197

E

Eagle Rare 169, 202
Early Times 12, 140, 141, 169
Edison, Thomas 199
Elijah Craig 164, 169, 214
Elmer T. Lee 126, 169
enzymes 54, 58, 203
esters 62, 72, 87, 102, 154, 208

ethanol 14, 62, 66, 70, 72, 75, 100, 104, 110, 111, 112, 158, 162, 205, 218
Evanston, Illinois 40
Evan Williams 164, 169
Evan Williams Bourbon Experience 42
Ezra Brooks 169

F

fermentation 56, 58, 62, 126, 204, 212, 216
FEW 40, 77, 201
Fields, W.C. 200
Fighting Cock 47, 169, 202
Fiore Distillery 20
Fisher, Terri 216
FitzSimmons, David 203, 218
flatboats 30, 199
Ford, Henry 199
Forged Oak 168
Forman, Louis 203
Four Roses 50, 64, 65, 77, 96, 119, 166, 168, 202, 204, 207, 215
Four Roses Bottling Facility 114
Four Roses Distillery 180, 204
Four Roses Single Barrel 204
Four Roses Small Batch 204
Four Roses Yellow Label 204
Frankfort, Kentucky 203
fungus 64, 112, 208
fusel oil 72

G

Garagiola, Joe 3
Garrison Brothers 21
George Dickel 12, 136, 138, 139, 168, 211
George Dickel Distillery 211
George T. Stagg 169, 209, 215
George T. Stagg Distillery 206, 210
gin 14
Glencairn glass 156, 213
Glenlivet 203
Glenmorange 55
glucose 203
grain 10, 14, 54, 58, 196, 197, 198, 201, 203, 205
grain neutral spirits 144, 211
Grant, Ulysses S. 209
Great Depression 36, 201

H

Hamilton, Alexander 26
Handelsman, Walt 198, 219
Havana Club 14
Hayden, Basil 210
heads 72, 74, 205
hearts 72, 75, 76
Heaven Hill 77, 166, 169, 202, 207, 214, 215, 218
Heaven Hill Distillery 178, 201, 215
Heavenhill, William 215
Henry McKenna 169
Hibiki 11
Hicks, Patrick 218
High West Distillery
    Campfire 165, 209, 214
    Son of Bourye 209
    Whiskey 209
    Yippee Ki-Yay 165, 214
high wine 75, 76, 205
Hillrock Estates 148, 212
Holmes Beach, Florida 218
Hoover, Herbert C. 201
Hurricane Hank's Liquors 218

I

Independent Stave Company 84, 206, 216, 218
Irish whiskey 10, 196, 209
Iron Smoke 212
I.W. Harper 47, 168, 202

J

Jack Daniel's 136, 137, 169, 206, 211
Jack Daniel's Distillery 138, 211
Jameson 11
Japanese whiskey 10, 196
Jarosick, Mike 208, 218
Jefferson's 119, 168, 202
Jefferson, Thomas 26, 198
jigger 162, 213
Jim Beam 77, 106, 168, 197, 202, 207, 210
    Black Label 103, 166
    Devil's Cut 117
    Ghost 103
    Repeal Batch 41, 201, 202, 209
    White Label 45, 103, 215
Jim Beam Distillery 170, 178, 208, 214
John J. Bowman 21, 49
Johnnie Walker 203
Johnny Drum 168

K

Kentucky bourbon 46, 202, 203, 214
Kentucky Bourbon Country: The Essential Travel Guide 216
Kentucky Bourbon Distillers LTD 168
Kentucky Bourbon Trail® 7, 186, 194, 216, 219
Kentucky Cooperage 84, 218
Kentucky Distiller's Association 216, 219, 221
Kentucky River 203, 215, 216
Kirin Brewing 168, 215
Knob Creek 47, 119, 151, 168, 202, 209, 210
Ku Klux Klan 200

L

Lang, Ryan 218
Laphroaig 203
Larceny 50, 127, 169, 210
Last Drop 212
Laurel Springs 3
Lawrenceburg Distillers Indiana 202
Leach, John A. 200
Lebanon, Kentucky 206, 207
Lee, Elmer T. 210
limestone 56, 203, 214
Lincoln, Abraham 198
Lincoln County Process 136, 138, 211
Louisville, KY 78
low wine 72, 76, 205
Lubbers, Bernie 128, 203, 210, 218
Luxco 169

M

Macallan 203
Maker's 46 152, 153
Maker's Mark 12, 13, 50, 77, 92, 106, 152, 166, 168, 196, 197, 202, 203, 205, 206, 207, 209, 215
Maker's Mark Distillery 176, 212
malt 160
maltose 203
mash bill 16, 50, 52, 64, 126, 140, 142, 147, 202, 203, 207, 212, 221
McDonald, John 209
McKenna 119
McKenzie 20, 209
medicinal whiskey 34, 38, 197, 200
Michelone Reserve 212
Michter's 45, 60, 77, 169, 202
Michter's US 1 Sour Mash 203
Middle West Spirits 22, 146, 204, 211, 218
Midwest Grain Products (MGP) 202
Milling, Elzy 218
Monkey Shoulder 55, 203
moonshine 38, 201, 205
Moonshine University 70, 205, 221
Moore, Turner C. 124
Morgan, J.P. 200
Morris, Chris 7, 160, 203, 204, 205, 210, 211, 213, 219
Mowry, Bob 218

N

NASCAR 200
Nation, Carrie 199
New Orleans 28, 29, 30, 198, 199, 217
Noah's Mill 127, 168, 210
Noe, Booker 171, 209
Noe, Fred 171
non-distiller producer 202

O

oak 10, 16, 44, 52, 78, 80, 84, 148, 150, 155, 196, 202, 203, 205, 206, 207, 212
O.F.C. Distillery 85, 206
Old Bardstown 168
Old Crow 168, 204
Old Ezra 12
Old Fitzgerald 50, 169
Old Forester 12, 50, 116, 117, 169, 198, 208
Old Forester President's Choice 210
Old Grand Dad 50, 127, 168, 210
Old Overholt 25, 197
Old Rip Van Winkle 124
Old Williamsburg 212
O'Neil, Elizabeth 204
orphan barrel 202
Oscar Pepper Distillery 204
Oyo 146, 212

P

Pappy Van Winkle 50, 77, 108, 124, 169, 203, 208, 218
pH 56, 60, 217
Prichard, Connie & Philip 218
Prichard's 138, 139, 211
Prichard's Double Barreled 152, 153
Prichard's Tennessee Whiskey 152, 218
Prohibition 32, 34, 36, 38, 40, 196, 197, 199, 200, 201, 215
proof 104, 111, 118, 132, 210
Pullman, George 199
Pure Food and Drug Act 1906 122
Pyccknn Ctahoapt 15

Q

Quercus 80, 205

R

rackhouse 96
Rebel Yell 50, 127, 169, 210
rectifiers 120, 210
Redemption 202
red layer 103, 206, 207
Red Stagg 212
Reigler, Susan 214, 218
Revolutionary War 24, 26, 199
rickhouse 94, 96, 98, 101, 104, 106, 108, 110, 111, 134, 203, 206, 207, 208, 209, 213, 215
Ridgemont Reserve's 1792 27, 166, 169, 198, 202
Rittenhouse 165
Rockefeller, John D. 199, 201
Rock Hill Farms 168
Roosevelt, Franklin D. 40, 201
Roosevelt, Teddy 122, 200
Rough Rider 45
Rowan's Creek 168
rum 14, 38, 197, 201

Russell, Jimmy 210
Russell's 122, 169, 210
Russell's Reserve Single Barrel 209
rye 10, 24, 26, 50, 54, 58, 147, 160, 197, 198, 203, 204, 211, 212

S

saccharification 203
Saccharomyces cerevisiae 64
Samuels, Bill 196
Samuels, Jr., Bill 194, 196
Samuels, Rob 196, 197
Samuels, T.W. 196
Sarasota, Florida 8, 124
Sazerac 11, 169, 214, 216
Scotch whiskey 10, 38, 196, 209
Seagram's 7 144, 145, 211
Seagram's Distillery 202, 215
secondary maturation 152
setback 60, 62, 66
Sinclair, Upton 122
single barrel 106, 118, 134, 207, 210
small batch 106, 118, 207, 209, 210
Smith, Kathy 205, 218
Smith, Teri 218
solera process 148
sour mash 60, 204
Southern Corn Whiskey 53
speed aging 154, 155
spirit safe 74, 205
Stagg Jr. 209
Standard of Identity 16, 18, 80, 211
starch 58, 203
Star Hill Farms 196
staves 30, 82, 84, 86, 90, 152, 154, 199, 206
Stave & Thief Society 220, 221
still
    Coffey 204
    column 66, 68, 205
    continuous 66, 204
    pot 42, 66, 68, 70, 76, 204
stillage 205
Stitzel-Weller Distillery 212
Straight Wheated Bourbon Whiskey 147, 211
Stranahan's Colorado Whiskey 60, 61, 165, 214
St. Valentine's Day massacre 201
sugar 62, 201, 203
sweet mash 60, 204, 212, 214
Sydnor, Davis 205

T

Taft, William H. 122, 210
tail box 74, 205
tails 72, 75, 205
Taylor, Edmund H. 120, 209, 215
Taylor, Zachary 209
Templeton 202
Ten High 8, 107, 144, 145, 169, 207
Tennessee whiskey 136, 138, 211
tequila 14, 38
Terressentia Corporation 154
Thousand Oaks Barrel Co. 8
thumper 76, 205
Tom Moore Bourbon 216
Town Branch 77, 126, 210
Twain, Mark 188

V

Van Winkle, Pappy 202
Van Winkle, Preston 208, 218
Van Winkle Rye 124
Vendome Copper and Brass Works 67, 204

Very Old Barton 50, 169
Vim & Petal 15
vodka 14, 70
Volstead Act 34, 40

W

Walgreen, Charles 200
warehouse 96, 134, 203
warehouse staining fungus 112, 208
Washington, George 26, 198, 219
water 10, 56, 58, 76, 110
Wathen's 202
Weller 50, 169, 202, 203
Western Citizen 198
wheat 50, 54, 58, 147, 160, 212
whiskey
  definition 10, 16
  rye 50, 197
  spelling 12, 196
  wheat 50, 146, 202
Whiskey Advocate 195
whiskey label 48, 209

Whiskey Obsession Festival 8, 124
Whiskey Rebellion 26, 198, 219
Whiskey Ring Scandal 209
Whisky Magazine 213, 219
WhistlePig 51
white dog 75, 76, 155
white lightning 52
Widow Jane 164, 212, 214
Wild Turkey 77, 132, 133, 166, 169, 202, 207, 208, 210
Wild Turkey 101 210
Wild Turkey Distilling Company 182, 216
Wild Turkey's American Honey 212
Willard, Frances Elizabeth 40, 201
Willett 168, 202, 210
Willett Distillery 94
Willett Pot Still 209
Willett Pot Still Reserve 68, 164, 204
William Wolf 150
Willis, Bruce 214

Wilson, Woodrow 32
wine 14, 199
W.L. Weller 51, 77, 209
Wolfram, Max 219
Women's Christian Temperance Union (WCTU) 32, 40, 199, 201
wood alcohol 36, 205
Woodford Reserve 6, 50, 68, 77, 166, 169, 202, 204, 205, 207, 208, 209, 219
Woodford Reserve Distillery 7, 174, 204
Woodford Reserve Double Oaked 152, 160, 164, 213
Woodford's Bourbon Academy 7
wort 204
Wray, Paul 205, 218
Wyoming Whiskey 20

Y

yeast 10, 58, 62, 64, 204, 215
Yellowstone 169

You can't judge a bourbon by its bottle, nevertheless, beauty comes in a variety of glassware that is both an art and craft, as is distilling. *Blood Oath Pact 3* is a blend of 7-year-old rye whiskey finished in cabernet-sauvignon barrels coupled with 7 and 12-year old ryed bourbon. *Bib & Tucker* is one of the few bourbons to come in a dark, embossed, flask-style bottle. "Made by Ghosts" is the catchy motto of *Boone County's* tribute to the early pioneer distillers of the county where bourbon was first produced in 1833. *Calumet Farm* is the home of eight Kentucky Derby winners: *Whirlaway, Pensive, Citation, Ponder, Hill Gail, Iron Liegh, Tim Tam,* and *Forward Pass.*

Bourbon Books by Acclaim Press

❖ *The Ambassador of Bourbon: Maker's Mark and the Rebirth of America's Native Spirit*
❖ *The Bourbon Tasting Notebook, Second Edition*
❖ *Buffalo Trace: Carving the Trail to Great Bourbon*
❖ *The Kentucky Bourbon Experience: A Visual Tour of Kentucky's Bourbon Distilleries*

WWW.ACCLAIMPRESS.COM • 877-427-2665